52

DEVOTIONS
TO FEED
YOUR FIRE

Soul Tending
for Youth Workers

Drew Dyson, editor

Contents

Introduction

Empty. Discouraged. Burned out. Restless. Turning the pages of the religious classifieds looking for the perfect job. Wandering the spirituality aisle of the bookstore looking for the perfect book. Surfing the web to plan the next vacation or spiritual retreat. All the while wondering where my passion had gone. My hunger and thirst for righteousness had been quenched by the empty calories of a busy calendar and an endless ministry "to-do" list.

I held the bread over the table and repeated the words that had become as routine as a trip to the 7-Eleven: "This is my body, broken for you." As I held the cup in the air, something happened. My fingers froze, my mouth was still, and my heart ached. Tears formed in my eyes as I forced out the words, "This is my blood . . ."

After the meal was served, the benediction pronounced, and the crowds dispersed, I knelt at the altar and began reading, "For the bread of God is that which comes down from heaven and gives life to the world. . . . I am the bread of life. Whoever comes to me will never go hungry, and whoever believes in me will never be thirsty" (John 6:33, 35). I consumed the remainder of the sacred meal with fervor as I continued to feast on the Word of God: "I am the living bread that came down from heaven. Whoever eats of this bread will live forever" (John 6:51).

This experience of emptiness was not my first, and such experiences are not unique to my journey. The very nature of ministry is the pouring out of self in order to meet the needs of others. Jesus poured out his life on the cross to open for all of humanity the "way that leads to life." You and I pour out our lives to serve the young people who wander into our youth rooms each week looking for manna from heaven to satisfy their ravenous hunger and emptiness.

So why didn't Jesus end up empty like we so often do? Because Jesus understood the importance of fullness. When his battery needed to be recharged, he withdrew to a quiet place to pray. When his soul was empty, he cried in prayer, "My God, My God." Even in times of despair and loneliness, Jesus was intimately connected to his Father.

Unlike Jesus, you and I often pour ourselves out when we are mostly empty. The overwhelming number of meetings, phone calls, football games, Bible studies, and lock-ins crowd out the time and energy needed to withdraw to a quiet place. The thunderous noise of our palm pilots and cell phones drowns out our ability to hear the still, small voice of God.

But there is good news and there is hope. When we feast on the Word of God, when we withdraw for moments of prayer and solitude, when we commit ourselves to the practices of faith, Jesus is there to offer us bread for life.

This book is not a collection of cute stories written by youth ministry experts whose first concern is selling books. This book is a collection of insights into the real-life struggles of ministry written by fellow companions on the journey who want to help feed your soul. Some of these companions are new to the journey and offer fresh insights and vital passion. Some are sages who offer years of wisdom that will guide us along our path.

But this book is just a side dish. The main course, the "bread of life," is God's Word made flesh—Jesus Christ. Only when you feast on him, when you dig deeply into the Word of God, will you experience the satisfaction of being filled to overflowing.

I pray that this book will become a conversation partner for your journey. In these pages you will find fresh perspectives on familiar dilemmas, probing questions that will push you into unexplored new territory, devotional readings that will breathe new life into dry bones, and reflections on Scripture that will open you to new ways of thinking. My prayer, ultimately, is that with or without this book you will discover, or re-discover the Bread of Life and that your hunger and thirst will be quenched.

Drew Dyson
Clinton, New Jersey

7 A Funny Thing Happened on the Way to Breakfast

> Let mutual love continue. Do not neglect to show
> hospitality to strangers, for by doing that some have
> entertained angels without knowing it.
>
> —Hebrews 13:1-2

It was a Christmas gift—a gift that we didn't use until eight months later. As a young youth pastor with very young children, my wife and I were thrilled to receive a night in an elegant Nashville hotel, brunch the next morning, and dinner at the kind of restaurant where they don't serve Happy Meals.® It had taken us so long to use the gift certificate; we were ready. We were excited about being together, just the two of us, with no agenda but each other.

But God had more than a second honeymoon in store for us. The night was all that we had hoped for. We dreamed about the future, laughed until our sides hurt, and pretended that we were falling in love for the first time all over again. But by 10:00 in the morning, knowing that our little vacation was coming to come to an end, we reluctantly headed down to breakfast.

When we sat down in the almost empty restaurant, our waiter introduced himself by drawing his name upside-down on the paper tablecloth. He introduced himself as "Mark from Kansas." We soon learned that he was a singer and songwriter who had just moved to Nashville, a city known for having the most talented waiters in the world.

We asked lots of questions. And since the restaurant was empty, he had plenty of time to talk. Each time he came to the table, he found a way to make us laugh. After Mark told us a bit about his faith, I let him know that our church was looking for a part-time youth director. "You wouldn't be interested, would you?" I asked. Mark was polite enough (after all, we hadn't left our tip yet), but it was clear that he could never see himself working with teenagers.

Mark knew that we were enjoying his tableside entertainment. By the end of the breakfast, he came to the table with a mischievous grin, carrying our check in one hand and a plate with two jalapeño peppers in the other. He challenged me to a contest: Whoever eats his pepper first without crying wins. (I lost.)

Before we left, we exchanged phone numbers, and in a few weeks, Mark and I were having lunch together. Soon he was in our home for a meal. (One of many times we fed the young man.) After lunch, he sat down at our upright piano and sang a song he had just written for his grandfather. That was the second time Mark Schultz made me cry.

Mark DeVries

Eventually, despite his resistance, I was able to persuade Mark to become the keyboard player for our youth choir. For the first six months that he performed in this role, he was able (amazingly) to hide the fact that he doesn't actually read music. Every few months, I would annoyingly ask him again to become our part-time youth director. And every few months he would let me know, in no uncertain terms, that he really needed to focus on his music.

But after keeping up with a group of highly caffeinated junior high boys on a ski trip (and enjoying it), I asked Mark to do the math. He was still working at the restaurant, often making even less than we could pay him as a youth director. And before we pulled into the church parking lot, he had begun his seven-year tenure working with the youth of our church.

For seven years Mark and I worked side-by-side helping kids get a clearer picture of Jesus. We traveled thousands of miles visiting and praying with our college students who were away at school; we embarrassed ourselves more than once with less-than-flattering skits; and we stood together with families in hospital rooms and at gravesides.

And all the while, Mark was writing songs. Some he wrote for our youth group to sing. Some he wrote about our kids and their families. Some he wrote for our worship services. Now it's hard to listen to Christian radio without hearing one of Mark's songs. And although he has sung his songs about our kids all around the country, it all began for us when we met this stranger at the Stouffer Hotel.

The Bible says that we should be careful how we treat strangers, since sometimes when we show hospitality to strangers, we are really "entertaining angels" without knowing it. It's hard for me now to meet strangers without wondering if a chance meeting might become a lifelong partnership in Jesus. But I draw the line at jalapeños.

Challenge: When you meet strangers today, pay attention. Ask them ten questions. Even as you are still talking to them, silently pray God's blessing over them.

Prayer: Lord, today let me be open to the strangers who you bring into my life. Help me honor each of them as if he or she were sent by you.

2 You Can Always Get There From Here

For by grace you have been saved through faith,
and this is not your own doing; it is the gift of
God—not the result of works, so that no one may boast. For we are
what he has made us in Christ Jesus for good works, which God
prepared beforehand to be our way of life.

—Ephesians 2:8-10

"You've got to know this one."

I played my brand new harmonica in my buddy Mark DeVries's ear—trying to help him relax. We were speeding down the highway in the wrong direction, and we knew it. We chose the east entrance ramp instead of the west one. And the next exit was twenty miles away. We had driven almost three thousand miles in seven days, had visited almost one hundred former youth group kids who were now college students, and we were lost again.

Nothing was particularly new about this situation. It seemed to happen every time we got into the car together. We'd pull out of a parking lot, and before long we'd be asking for directions. "Sign? What sign? Turn left by the pack of Elk? What?" This particular evening we had a midnight appointment to meet with a college student who was still a couple hundred miles away. Every mile we drove took us further from where we were going.

I could tell that DeVries was getting tense. So I figured that playing a few rounds of "Name That Tune" with my new harmonica would help both of us relax a little. But despite the quality of my playing and variety of my song selections, I could see no signs of relaxation on my friend's face. In fact, the more I played, the tighter Mark gripped the steering wheel, the whiter his knuckles got, and the more his jaw clenched. (I guess driving three thousand miles with a harmonica player will do that to someone.)

I've learned a few things since those days. Now, when I rent a car, I always try to get one of those talking maps. You've probably heard of them. They are called GPS systems (Global Positioning Systems), and they actually track the exact location of your car from a satellite. You enter your destination, and as you approach each turn, the system actually speaks to you through a little box inside your car. "Turn left, one hundred feet."

One day I was driving a rental car by myself. The GPS system was working perfectly. It warned me that my next turn was coming up. I don't know if I was missing the days of being lost with my buddy or if I was just feeling a little

Mark Schultz

mischievous, but I decided to try a little experiment. So far the GPS had told me correctly everything from how to back out of the parking stall to how to merge onto the highway. This thing can't be that good, I thought.

So I decided to see if I could get the GPS lost and confused. When it said, "Exit right, one hundred feet," I skipped the exit on purpose. The screen on the little box froze for a second and then went completely dark. I had won! I had outsmarted this little box. I could get the GPS box lost as easily as I could get DeVries lost. YES! Just as I was about to pull out my harmonica for a celebrative rendition of "We Are the Champions," it happened: The screen lit up and popped back on with a chime. It had recalculated my route and had figured another way to get me where I was supposed to go.

That box's voice is a whole lot like another voice—a voice that I want to listen to more than any other. Like the GPS, God's voice doesn't scold me for making a stupid, rebellious, or stubborn choice. Even when I choose not to follow, God is already providing me with the quickest route to where God wants me to be. (And God does it faster than a GPS.) No matter how many wrong turns we make, we cannot walk off the map of God's love for us.

Sometimes I get lost accidentally. And sometimes, I'm embarrassed to admit, I get lost on purpose. But God is never confused about where I am. And God is never confused about getting me back on the right track. Today's Scripture tells us that God has already prepared work ahead of time for us to do. No matter where you are or how far you may have wandered from God's path, you can always "get there from here."

But take my advice: Leave the harmonica at home.

Challenge: When you feel the pressure coming on and you are deciding how to get back on track, test your words and actions with this question: "Will taking this step put me closer to God's destination for me or further away from it?"

> Prayer: Lord, I want to follow your quiet voice. Whether I'm hopelessly lost or walking in the center of your will, teach me to be responsive to you, to learn to say yes to your promptings.

This devotion was inspired by a sermon by Dr. Tony Evans.

3 After the Earthquake

Be strong and bold; have no fear or dread of
them, because it is the Lord your God who goes
with you; he will not fail you or forsake you.

—Deuteronomy 31:6

In 1989 an earthquake hit Armenia (a small Christian nation that was then part of the Soviet Union). The quake flattened cities and killed more than thirty thousand people in minutes. In one city, after the shaking had stopped, a young couple looked around as relief flooded their faces. Their house was in shambles, but they were both still alive.

No sooner had the relief come than they remembered their young son, Armand, who had gone off to school that morning. The father made sure his wife was safe then headed off for his son's school. Moving as quickly as his feet could carry him, he kept remembering the promise he made to his son as a regular bedtime ritual: "Son, remember that I will always be there for you."

The father's heart sank when he saw what was left of the school building. It was flattened. He needed a few minutes to get his bearings, to determine where his son's classroom would have been. He made his best guess of where to begin and started pulling rocks away from the rubble.

The other parents who had gathered at the school—many wailing and crying—said to this father: "You know there's no use. Leave it alone. It's too late."

He looked at each parent and asked, "Will you help me?"

They all looked at him and simply answered, "There's nothing to be done. It's dangerous here. Just go home and get some rest."

But this father ignored them and continued, pulling one rock at a time off of the endless pile of debris.

Fire fighters came with warnings that fires had broken out all over the city. They too encouraged the father to go home. But the father stayed and urged the fire fighters to help him find his son. They replied, "We have to hurry to help those who can still be saved. Go home where it is safe. Get some rest."

But the father just returned to his pile of rocks. He continued pulling rocks away for five hours straight. Five hours turned to ten and ten turned into twenty-four, then thirty, then thirty-six. After thirty-six hours, he heard a voice. He screamed the name of his son, "Armand!"

Mark DeVries and Mark Schultz

With new intensity, the father pushed boulders and rocks out of the way, all the while calling his son's name. Then the impossible happened. From a small gap between rocks, the father could hear a faint voice, "Dad?"

The father, now frantic, continued calling his son's name, pulling rock after rock away. He called out, "Son, are you OK?"

He was close enough to hear his son now. The boy said, "There are fourteen out of thirty-three of us left, and we are hungry and thirsty. But I knew you would come. I told the other kids that if my dad was alive, he'd be here."

Widening the hole enough for a child's body to fit through, the father reached his long arm down and called out, "Son, reach up and let me pull you out."

"No, dad," his son answered. "Take the other kids first, because I know you'll be there for me."

When you find yourself waiting for God and wondering why it seems like the Lord is absent from your life, remember that we have a God who will never leave us nor forsake us, a God who will go to desperate lengths to demonstrate just how much we are loved.

Challenge: Cling to God's promise today, and repeat it to yourself every hour: "I will never leave you nor forsake you." Choose one person for whom you can demonstrate the persistent love of God simply by being there for him or her.

Prayer: Lord, sometimes I feel like I'm buried under emotions that overwhelm me, under responsibilities that consume me, under the weight of mistakes that paralyze me. During those times, I'm tempted to assume that I am the farthest thing from your mind. But Lord, as I wait in the darkness, I trust that you have not forgotten me nor forsaken me; and I rest in knowing that you will find me and restore me again.

4 Who Is in Your Balcony?

Therefore, since we are surrounded by so great a
cloud of witnesses, let us also lay aside every
weight and the sin that clings so closely, and let
us run with perseverance the race that is set before us,
looking to Jesus the pioneer and perfecter of our faith.
—Hebrews 12:1-2a

It was high school graduation time—I was getting ready for my eighth graduation of the season. Since the young woman I was coming to see walk the stage had a last name that started with "S," I knew that I could be late. So I snuck into the balcony after the ceremony had already started.

But this was not any balcony. This was at the Ryman Auditorium, the home of country music. This auditorium was built by a riverboat captain who had been converted. He wanted to create a revival hall, a place where as many people as possible could be as close to the front as possible. So this balcony was unique.

Unlike many auditorium balconies that rest quietly against the back wall, this balcony was almost as large as the bottom floor seating area. In fact only a few pews (the Ryman still has pews) on the floor level are not covered by the massive balcony. A person sitting in the front row of the balcony actually feels closer to the stage than the person in the front row of the floor level.

So there I sat in the back of the balcony. Though I was at least an hour late, the school officials still had not even begun handing out diplomas. They were giving out awards. Finally, they came to the all-around award, the award given to the one person in the school who most exemplified its values.

The more they talked about the young man who had won the award, the more interested I became. The speaker said, "Our award winner tonight was born in Russia, and though some doctors thought he would never walk, he ran on our track team. When he moved here at the age of ten, he knew very little English; but today he is graduating from high school with honors. This coming year, he will be traveling to Israel to begin his studies to be a rabbi."

The crowd sat calmly in their seats and clapped politely, as though a golfer had just sunk a three-inch putt. But on the front row of the balcony was one who couldn't stay seated. This large, elderly man—apparently the boy's grandfather—stood tall on the front row of that grand balcony, his full white beard framing his rugged face. Not only did he stand, but he slowly, almost majestically, placed his arms in the air in celebration, perhaps in worship, maybe both. He was the boy's ancient, unembarrassed fan club of one.

Someone has said that for kids to make the transition to adulthood successfully, they need people in their lives who are "crazy about them," who are willing to love them irrationally, even when doing so may be embarrassing. I would guess that this grandfather was just that kind of influence in his grandson's life. And I have to believe that this grandfather had been in such a position before. When the child was born and the family feared he would be crippled for life, I'm guessing this grandfather was praying. When this child moved to this frightening, foreign land when he was just ten years old, I can only bet that his grandfather was crying out to God for his boy.

You may already be blessed with a "Jewish grandfather" in your balcony, or maybe you have a whole family of them. If you do, thank God; and thank them for believing in you on the days when you can't believe in yourself. If you don't yet have these people in your life, there is much that you can do.

Make the decision to "stack the stands" for yourself. Start with the people in your church who are old enough to be grandparents. Talk to them, learn about their life, and invite them to pray you through your life. Few other investments you can make will pay richer dividends than filling your balcony with "Jewish grandfathers."

When the Bible talks about these kinds of folks, it calls them a "great cloud of witnesses." We all run our race of faith better when we are surrounded by the right people. Who's in your balcony?

Challenge: Make a list of everyone in your "cloud of witnesses"—those persons who encourage you in your faith. Think of people you know or have heard about, people who are living or passed. Next, make a list of all the people whose "cloud of witnesses" you are in—people you offer encouragement to as they run their race.

Prayer: Thank you, Lord, for surrounding me with a great cloud of witnesses. Thank you especially for those whom I have never noticed before. I want to live into the prayers they have prayed for me. And Lord, help me to be in the stands for others, to encourage them, and to call out your best in them.

5 Biker on a Mission

Not that I have already . . . reached the goal;
but I press on to make it my own, because Christ
Jesus has made me his own. Beloved, I do not
consider that I have made it my own; but this one
thing I do: forgetting what lies behind and straining forward
to what lies ahead. I press on toward the goal for the prize of
the heavenly call of God in Christ Jesus.

—Philippians 3:12-14

I could hardly breathe. My bike rested against an evergreen tree; I was bent over with my hands on my knees. When I found the strength to look up, I looked back down the slope of the mountain we had just conquered. My head pounded; my legs throbbed; I wondered if I was going to pass out. Then someone behind me called out the good news: "Let's take a quick break, there's an even bigger one up ahead of us!"

"Bigger? Did he say BIGGER?"

I was raised in Kansas, for crying out loud. We don't have mountains there. It baffled me. Why did God go and put mountains right here in the middle of our bike route?

Nine months earlier, I had joined six other men from our church as we rallied around one of our team members whose fourteen-year-old son, Martin, had been diagnosed with leukemia. We were all looking for a way to do something productive to help fight Martin's cancer.

A hundred-mile bike ride had sounded easy enough back then, even kind of enchanting. But that was when I was reclining in my strat-o-lounger in front of the television, drinking a Pepsi® with a deep-dish pizza box laying across my chest. (Almost anything seems enchanting from that position!)

Actually putting the rubber to the road was an entirely different matter. Training rides on early mornings, cold mornings, and blistering hot afternoons left my sore muscles screaming in unison and me wondering many days if I would be able to lift my aching body out of bed.

I'll tell you right now that you don't feel any of that pain from a recliner. But staying in the recliner would have meant that I would have had to stay away from this mission my friends and I had chosen together.

So there I was, forty miles into a hundred-mile bike race through the mountains of Lake Tahoe, each mile raising money for cancer research. Our

Mark Schultz

performance in the actual race was a far cry from our first embarrassed training day months earlier, when we all stood around self-consciously in our skintight spandex suits and oversized crash helmets feeling awkward—like big kids going through puberty again.

For months, we trained together, wrecked together, fixed flats together, and laughed and sang together. We came a long, long way, all for a clear purpose, one bigger than any one of us, a purpose that could never be realized without encouragement from one another.

Crossing the finish line late that afternoon felt like riding through the gates of heaven. Our group of otherwise quite ordinary men (Team Advil®, as we affectionately called ourselves) had done something extraordinary as we crossed that line together—singing.

The following spring, the team began training again. Unfortunately, my traveling schedule prevented me from making the training rides, and I gave up my spot to a replacement rider. Team Advil® couldn't possibly have found a better one. Besides the fact that he was a good seventy-five pounds lighter than me, he brought one other quality to the table that inspired the team to train harder and raise more pledges than they ever could have done with me. He had been there.

Their replacement rider had never ridden such distance on a bike, but he had ridden the wild, demanding ride of chemotherapy and recovery. I've seen the race-finishing picture that hangs on the wall of my friend's home: Six middle-aged men in spandex following behind fifteen-year-old Martin, cured of cancer, leading his dad and his team toward the finish line, singing of course.

Tired, humbled, and deeply satisfied, they finished well.

Challenge: Choose one spiritual discipline that you want to practice regularly this year as part of your training for finishing the race of faith you have begun.

Prayer: Thank you, Lord, for calling me into this wild ride of following you. When I feel like I can't go another mile, give me courage not to give up. When I feel like I'm alone, remind me of those you've called to ride alongside me. And when I am obsessed with my own journey, lift my eyes to see those you are calling me to serve.

6 Reckless Truth

I will sing to the Lord all my life;
    I will sing praise to my God as long as I
    live.
May my meditation be pleasing to him,
    as I rejoice in the Lord.
But sinners may vanish from the earth,
    and the wicked be no more.
Praise the Lord, O my soul.
Praise the Lord.

—Psalm 104:33-35, NIV
(Read Psalm 104)

The Bible is a reckless book. It speaks God's truth to us completely, honestly, and with little regard for whether we like it, how it makes us feel, or how it might disrupt our precious ideas about the way life works. The Bible makes no attempt to smooth out the rough parts or play down the hard parts. It's just all there as it is.

Psalm 104 is an example of such ruthless honesty. The psalm regales in God's greatness—the majesty, the wondrous works, and the gracious provision of a loving Creator. The psalmist's praise cascades through the verses, gratitude splashing off almost every word.

It opens, "How many are your works, O LORD?" It closes thirty-five verses later with the summary exclamation, "Praise the LORD!" It is nothing less than an anthem from beginning to end.

Perhaps that's why many of us are a little embarrassed by the phrase tucked away in verse 35: "Let sinners be consumed from the earth, and let the wicked be no more." Like a ransom letter sitting on a rack next to the greeting cards, the verse seems oddly out of place—a little bit rough and rude and shockingly raw. Of course, the psalms are not greeting cards. The psalms are not just the sentimental stuff of needlework and wall plaques. The Book of Psalms was the prayer book of the people of Israel, real people like us who felt precisely these kinds of mixed sentiments and conflicting passions everyday.

Let's be honest: Some of us feel all of these emotions—joy, thankfulness, anger, confusion—just in the course of one typical night at youth group! We sort of start off the evening thinking, "O LORD, how manifold are your works" (verse 24a)! But about halfway through the meeting, it's, "Let sinners be consumed from the earth" (verse 35a)!

Duffy Robbins

Challenge: The rough edge of Psalm 104 is the double-edged sword that poses this basic question:

> We are quite willing to praise God as the Lord of Creation, but are we as willing to admit that God also must remake us?

Sometimes revelation is what God shows us through nature. And sometimes revelation is what God shows us about our own nature.

Prayer: Lord, help me to move beyond a "greeting card sentimentality" to see real life in real terms. Grant me open eyes, open ears, and an open heart that I might become more aware of the rough edges of my life and ministry—even when they are crude, ugly, and a little bit shocking.

7 The Miracle of Thirst

O God, you are my God,
   earnestly I seek you;
my soul thirsts for you,
   my body longs for you,
in a dry and weary land
   where there is no water.

—Psalm 63:1, NIV

Thirst is one of those bodily warning signs that we take for granted. We don't feel gratitude for the headache that prods us to consume more liquids or the "dry mouth" that prompts us to take a sip of water.

Thirst is just one more bodily mechanism. On a good day we don't give even a moment of thought to the gift of thirst. And yet, if we are to believe what medicine tells us, this capacity for thirst is a vital and wonderful blessing. Thirst tells us something very important about ourselves. Survival specialists suggest that this gauge is the one we most need to monitor in the wilderness. It is possibly the most important warning light on our body's dashboard.

In light of this fact Jesus' claim to be the source of "living water" (John 7:37-39) becomes especially significant. Jesus reminds us that, just as thirst warns us of physical need, another mechanism makes us aware of spiritual needs. That mechanism is a God-given thirst for what only God can supply: the Holy Spirit in us, filling us with streams of living water.

It is striking that Jesus mentions this spiritual thirst on the "last and greatest day of the Feast" (John 7:37)—a time when most people's bodily gauges were on "full." By delivering such a message in such a setting, Jesus says that, in the midst of all of this fullness, some yet thirst.

Youth ministry can easily become a feast of activities, appointments, talks, and meetings. But how often in the midst of this fullness do we still feel a deep inner thirst? Maybe we aren't running on empty, but we sure aren't running on full. If you feel that way today, perhaps you should heed the warnings on your spiritual dashboard.

This thirst for living water is a miraculous gift of God. It is a gracious invitation from a God who says to us, "When you have tried to fill yourself with every other morsel of the world's feast and still find yourself thirsty? Listen. Jesus says, "Come to me and drink."

Duffy Robbins

Challenge: Today, before you get caught up in another day of the youth ministry feast, take some time to read the Word (see Psalm 63), sing a hymn, and take a long refreshing drink from the presence of your Heavenly Father.

Prayer: O Lord, my soul yearns for you; my spirit thirsts for you in a dry and weary land where there is no water. Help me, Lord, to seek you this day. You are the one true source for my refreshment—not a great meeting, not more kids coming to youth group, not an appointment that goes well, not a parent who calls to thank me or a pastor who drops me a note of appreciation— just you, the Living Water.

8 Calling or Career?

Then they asked him, "What must we do to do the works God requires?" Jesus answered, "The work of God is this: to believe in the one he has sent."

—John 6:28-29, NIV

More and more these days, we hear people talk about choosing youth ministry as a career. Maybe this view of youth ministry is a step up, but is it a step in the right direction?

The English word *career* comes from the French *carriere*, meaning a road, or a highway. Think of someone setting out on a road, map in hand, with a goal in sight. The word *calling* or *vocation*, on the other hand, from the Latin word *vocare*, points neither to a map, nor a guidebook, but to the Guide. Calling, unlike career, emphasizes not following a course but responding to a voice. A calling is not determined by a schedule, an itinerary, or well-laid plans. From beginning to end, the key to being called is maintaining an open, intimate relationship with the One whose voice speaks.

Why should this distinction matter to you today? Because how you view yourself as a youth worker is, at some level, rooted in whether you are pursuing a career or a calling. In fact, it was precisely this mistake that almost led Moses to forsake his calling. When God spoke to him from the burning bush (Exodus 3), Moses responded as if God were interviewing him about a career choice: He had been employed as a sheep-farmer; how would he like to consider moving into delivery work? And Moses asked reasonable questions:

• Did God suppose that he was really qualified for this kind of work?

• Did God really feel that he had the proper experience, the right skills for such a task?

• Didn't God know that he was a poor public speaker?

• What if the people didn't follow him?

• What if they just thought he was some yahoo from the sticks who had come to the big city with his hot rod?

Moses' questions were all very reasonable if the issue were career choices. And they're the kind of questions we, as youth workers, all ask ourselves everyday. Am I fit for this job? Am I young enough? Cool enough? Funny enough? Athletic enough? What must I do today to convince people that I'm "doing my job"?

Duffy Robbins

But those kinds of questions are not nearly as scary or intimidating when we realize that the key issue in ministry is not suitability to a career, but sensitivity to a call. "You did not choose me, but I chose you to go and bear fruit—fruit that will last" (John 15:16, NIV).

Youth ministry: It's not a job; it's an adventure!

Challenge: How would your day change if you made a conscious effort to approach ministry as a calling instead of a career? Would it change your schedule? Would it change the way you approach various items on your schedule? What if today's responsibilities were as much about listening as about doing?

Prayer: Thank you, Lord, for reminding me again that what you really care about in my ministry is not what I *do*, but who I *am*. Help me, Lord, to cultivate the art of listening for a calling instead of worrying about a career.

9 Fresh Ministry Served Here?

This is what the LORD says—
  he who made a way through the sea,
  a path through the mighty waters,
who drew out the chariots and horses,
  the army and reinforcements together,
and they lay there, never to rise again,
  extinguished, snuffed out like a wick:
"Forget the former things;
  do not dwell on the past.
See, I am doing a new thing!
  Now it springs up; do you not perceive it?
I am making a way in the desert
  and streams in the wasteland."

—Isaiah 43:16-19, NIV

Stale youth ministry, like stale bread, will not just taste crummy. In time it will start to crumble and fall apart. And when that happens, it leaves a bad taste in everybody's mouth—leaders and kids alike. That's why effective youth ministry is born of freshness. But, freshness has a lot of cheap imitations:

- <u>Sometimes novelty is mistaken for freshness.</u> Instead of fresh bread we serve new recipes for the latest spirituality cooked up by some new age chef who has a twist that will make the gospel a little easier to swallow.

- <u>Sometimes spontaneity is mistaken for freshness.</u> Instead of fresh bread served thoughtfully with a balanced nutritional program of Bible study, small groups, relationships, and fun—a ministry driven by a biblical vision—we just sort of "let the Spirit lead" with the attitude that "whatever happens, happens." The bad news is that what usually happens with that kind of spontaneity is not fresh programming but half-baked programming.

- <u>Sometimes bells and whistles are mistaken for freshness.</u> We try to "up" the youth budget so that we can buy some cool new technology or add a new sound system or renovate a crumbling youth room. But it turns out that fresh bread is not about raising more dough. And stale bread, even when it's eaten in a nice new dining room, still tastes stale.

Part of the wonder of an encounter with Christ is that he brings freshness out of staleness—dead, dull eyes, come alive with a splash of color and light; frail, dried up limbs become moving, twisting, living forms.

Duffy Robbins

In the book of Isaiah God declares, "I am doing a new thing! Now it springs up; do you not perceive it?" (43:19, NIV).

But there is a difference between new and fresh. The youth ministry world is dazzled by new and novel ideas and technologies. If it's new and edgy, we like it. But our hunger for the new can sometimes starve us of substance and staples.

Challenge: For two thousand years of church history, the church has grown through fellowship, worship, service, and the apostles' teachings. This is not a plea for stodginess and tradition. Stale bread is just as unhealthy as raw batter. But, it is a reminder, as you look at your ministry today, this week, this month, to pray over this question: Am I feeding my students the fresh bread of life, or just some half-baked novelty?

Prayer: Lord, guide me in my ministry and renew me in my heart, that I might not fall into the trap of offering novelty as an insubstantial substitute for freshness.

10 The Call of the Wild

"I am sending you out like sheep among wolves. Therefore be as shrewd as snakes and as innocent as doves. Be on guard against men; they will hand you over to the local councils and flog you in their synagogues. On my account you will be brought before governors and kings as witnesses to them and to the Gentiles. But when they arrest you, do not worry about what to say or how to say it. At that time you will be given what to say, for it will not be you speaking, but the Spirit of your Father speaking through you. . . .

"A student is not above his teacher, nor a servant above his master. It is enough for the student to be like his teacher."

—Matthew 10:16-20, 24, NIV
(*Read Matthew 10:16-24*)

Parker Palmer, in his book, *The Courage to Teach* (Jossey-Bass, 1997), opens with these words: "I am a teacher at heart, and there are moments in the classroom when I can hardly hold the joy. When my students and I discover uncharted territory to explore, when the pathway out of a thicket opens up before us, when our experience is illumined by the lightning-life of the mind—then teaching is the finest work I know" (page 1).

Those of us in youth ministry—those of us who step into a Sunday school classroom or in front of a group of teenagers each week as a leader or teacher—hopefully have come to know something of that privilege. Most of us can also appreciate Palmer's sense of adventure, discovering with our students "uncharted territory to explore, when the pathway out of a thicket opens up before us."

I love using that imagery of adventure to describe what we do in youth ministry. That language says something, first of all, about the importance of our role as the expedition leader. It is we who have walked the trail before. It is we who have some sense of the most enticing vistas, and we who have some sense of the most dangerous trouble spots. It is we who understand best the ups and downs of the trail ahead, and it is we who perhaps best appreciate what it takes to be outfitted for such a journey. It is we who get the joy of shared adventures, and we who feel most deeply the loss of those who begin the journey but do not choose to finish.

But, the adventure imagery also reminds us that we are still on a journey and that there are unknowns and risks ahead. Adventure, by definition, involves risk. None of us knows precisely where this trail will lead us—what investments it will require, what challenges it will bring.

It's an amazing, messy, wonderful, demanding adventure.

The one mistake we must not make in this endeavor is to play it safe. Bungee jumping is an adventure. Using bungee cords to tie everything down tight is just a job. It's that mysterious unknown that makes youth ministry interesting.

Challenge: In an age of increased emphasis on technique, know-how, and strategy, let us beware of shrinking down God's amazing call into "three simple steps," "five clear stages," or "six snappy ideas." If our work isn't dangerous, we probably aren't approaching it right. Jesus called us to explore a wild kingdom, not sit and enjoy an amusement park ride through Jungle Land.

Prayer: Lord, be with me, for you know that I am sometimes a person of timid heart and tamed appetites. Deliver me, Jesus, from a ministry that shrinks back from risk and turns away from the big adventure to which you've called me.

11) Not Really Suited for the Task at Hand?

When thinking through the trials and hassles that face us as youth workers, it's pretty easy to get discouraged. If you've been in youth ministry more than twenty minutes you know this job can be hard work. Who are we to think that we might be qualified for such a teaching assignment?

One of my favorite stories of exploration is the story of the 1869 expedition in which ten men successfully navigated the Colorado River through the entire course of the Grand Canyon for the very first time. Edward Dolnick's recent account, *Down the Great Unknown* (Perennial, 2002), is a classic study of grit, courage, determination, and good fortune. But what most attracts me to the story is that the expedition leader, John Wesley Powell—described by Dolnick as "a professor at a no-name college...small and scrawny...a stick of beef jerky adorned with whiskers" (page 1)—was a man with only one arm. How remarkable that a one-armed man was the leader of the first rowing expedition through this treacherous stretch of whitewater snaking its way through the towering walls of the Grand Canyon.

And how encouraging!

Maybe it's just me, but as a youth worker I confess that I often feel like a one-armed man in a two-oared boat. Helping kids navigate the rapids and danger spots of their teenage years, I often feel as if I am quite literally short-handed. I am not, in fact, lacking a right arm, but I am well aware of areas in which I am lacking. Who of us doesn't have this deep sense that we're just one Bible study disaster or one youth group debacle from "man overboard"?

To those of you reading this book who feel a little short-handed in your ministry with kids, let me remind you that we are not in this boat alone. Christ is taking the other oar, and our insufficiency is where we discover his sufficiency. The adventure of ministry has never been about capable people launching into a work for which they were completely prepared. It's about people of strong heart and courageous faith willing to set sail with Jesus and trust him to lead "down the great unknown."

Maybe that's what the Apostle Paul was talking about when he wrote:

But we have this treasure in jars of clay to show that this all-surpassing power is from God and not from us. We are hard pressed on every side, but not crushed; perplexed, but not in despair; persecuted, but not abandoned; struck down, but not destroyed. . . .

Duffy Robbins

Therefore we do not lose heart. Though outwardly we are wasting away, yet inwardly we are being renewed day by day. For our light and momentary troubles are achieving for us an eternal glory that far outweighs them all. So we fix our eyes not on what is seen, but on what is unseen. For what is seen is temporary, but what is unseen is eternal.

—2 Corinthians 4:7-8, 16-18, NIV

<u>Challenge: In what part of your ministry do you feel a little short-handed today? Is it ability? staffing? facility? Whatever it is, give thanks to God for the assurance today that you are not alone at the oars.</u>

Prayer: Thank you, Lord, that your power is made perfect in my weakness (2 Corinthians 12:9).

12 My Mother Told Me There Would Be Days Like This

"He has blocked my way so that I cannot pass;
    he has shrouded my paths in darkness.
He has stripped me of my honor
    and removed the crown from my head.
He tears me down on every side till I am gone;
    he uproots my hope like a tree.
His anger burns against me;
    he counts me among his enemies. . . .

"Oh, that my words were recorded,
    that they were written on a scroll,
that they were inscribed with an iron tool on lead,
    or engraved in rock forever!
I know that my Redeemer lives,
    and that in the end he will stand upon the earth.
And after my skin has been destroyed,
    yet in my flesh I will see God;
I myself will see him
    with my own eyes—I, and not another.
    How my heart yearns within me!"

—Job 19:8-11, 23-27, NIV

There are days when the mother of one of your most problematic students is waiting for you when you get to work. These will probably be the same days when there are extra long lines at the coffee shop and when you forget the budget request in your home computer so that you have had to turn around and go back. You arrive to work late and she is waiting for you.

There are days when your boss calls you at home to say, "I'd like to see you tomorrow, I know it's your day off but we need to discuss something."

There are days when you put hours into a lesson, and in the first five minutes one of your girls says to another across the room "I know who likes you." From that point on it's not your lesson anymore.

Every complaint you get is for a reason. Every kid who decides that he or she doesn't want to work on the mission trip is there for a reason. Every staff meeting . . . . (OK, maybe not those.) But just about *every*thing that happens to you in your job happens for a reason. The good days and the bad days and the days when you just show up.

Steve Case

Youth ministers are a strange lot. We want to please God. I mean we really *really* want to please God and yet it seems like there are some days when everything that gets thrown in our path comes crashing down like the semi-truck in the movie *Twister*. This is youth ministry. There is no other option. There is no time to map out another plan. There are days we must simply get through.

Read Psalm 27. You would almost think David was a youth minister. There is something that lives deep down inside of you. Down past your doubts and fears. Down past your needs and frailties. It shouts loudly to be heard above the voices that ring in your ears that ask you, "Why are you doing this job, again?"

It is a love. It is a deep abiding love for teenagers that God placed there long before you became a youth minister. God put it there sometime when you were a teenager, when you were so self-absorbed that you didn't know it was being installed. Now it grows. It beats like your heart. It lives and breathes inside of you so that when you finally shut out the complainers and the budgets and the apathetic, you will hear it. You will see that one kid who sat in the back of the room and didn't participate. You will hear that kid who keeps doing an impression of his alcoholic father. You will catch that glance that says "I need to talk to someone." And you will smell the coffee and the donuts as you sit across from that lost soul who can't figure out where her life is going or why people treat her the way they do or why mom said *that* or why that boy laughs to his friends when she passes by him in the hall. And you will understand. And you will listen. And you will comfort and you will advise. And you will do all of these things out of the earshot and eyesight of your biggest detractors. Because you are not in this job for them. You are in this job for the kid who sits across the table from you and pours herself out. And you will help her get through.

Prayer: God of Creation, lift us out of this hole. Give a shield. Cover us with your love. Put your hands over our ears so the words don't hurt. We are your servants. You never promised us this would be easy, you only promised to be with us no matter what we went through. We need you now, God. We need to be absolutely sure of your presence. We need to know we are not talking to the ceiling. Give us faith. Give us hope. Give us your love. Amen.

13 Fix My Kid

"Lord, if it's you," Peter replied, "tell me to come to you on the water."

"Come," he said.

Then Peter got down out of the boat and walked on the water to Jesus. But when he saw the wind, he was afraid and, beginning to sink, cried out, "Lord, save me!"

Immediately, Jesus reached out his hand and caught him. "You of little faith," he said, "why did you doubt?"

—Matthew 14:28-31, NIV

It is always amazing to think of the kinds of teenagers that show up to a youth meeting. Many times you see kids who refuse to participate, refuse to talk, refuse to smile, and often refuse to stay awake. These youth are there because mom and dad make them come. Or maybe one kid just got arrested, and, as part of his probation, he has agreed to become more involved in his church (which means that he comes to youth group and just sits there for an hour.)

Often Mom and Dad have no idea what to do with their teenager. They are at their wits end. They can't make their daughter behave. She's defiant. She's moody. She's disobedient. She's rude. She's disrespectful. Mom and Dad think, "Hey, there's a youth minister at the church. Maybe *he* can fix her. Let's make her go to church."

So mom and dad drive up to the church on a Sunday night—barely slowing down enough to let their daughter off at the door before roaring off, glad to have an evening to themselves without the arguing and the yelling and the frustration. So their daughter sits in the youth room, sullen and withdrawn and staring at you with eyes that say, "Go ahead. Fix me."

Ready for some news? You can't fix a kid. You cannot take the irritable teenager who was once the precious child of the couple that just threw gravel in your parking lot and turn her into the adoring child he or she once was. You can't do it.

When parents say "Fix my kid," they usually mean, "Make our kid more like us." Some of the greatest tension in homes comes when the parents think, "He's not like us. There must be something wrong with him. Why doesn't he just grow up?" Sometimes you just have problem kids. But *you cannot fix them*. You'll just be banging your head on the wall if you try.

Here's what you can do: You can listen. You can watch. You can offer consistency. Consistency is a wonderful gift to give someone whose life never

Steve Case

seems to have any. You and your Wednesday night M&M®-fest may be the only structure a kid has. Teenage life is full of day-to-day (even second-to-second) changes. You can plant seeds. Johnny may sit on the youth couch with his arms crossed for four years and then go off to college and you'll think, "I never reached him." Not true. You planted seeds.

Too often as youth workers we think of ourselves as the one standing out on the water saying "Come." But, that job's already been filled. The oft-used phrase, "You are the only Jesus that some people will ever see," is just too scary to think about sometimes.

But we can sit in the boat. *That* is our job. We sit in the boat and offer encouragement. We put a reassuring hand on our students' shoulders. We say supportive words. But when it comes right down to it, the decision to step out of the boat belongs to them. Jesus didn't pull Peter out of the boat. Peter had to make the decision to take the step. And Jesus did not reach out and grab Peter until he got scared and started sinking. Those in your youth group must make the same decision to step out. You can't make it for them. Once Peter took that step, his life changed forever. That's scary. That's what keeps so many of us in the boat. "My life will change, and I'll never be the same." Who wouldn't be scared? But the worst thing you can do is push a kid out of the boat. You may want to sometimes, but you cannot shove or drag a teenager into the waiting arms of Jesus. You cannot fix a kid.

You can sit with these youth. Encourage them. Be there to hold them when they get back in the boat soaking wet with the love of Jesus and scared out of their wits. You can also sit by them when they decide not to get out of the boat. You can encourage them then too. You can hold them when they are scared then too. That is what we do as youth ministers. We are not Jesus but we can point to the guy standing out there on the waves and say, "It's OK. I'll be here when you get back."

Prayer: God of miracles. We need one down here right about now. People don't see the frustrations and the disappointments that go along with this job. We want our students to know you. We may feel angry, hurt, or dissatisfied; but we never feel like we are alone. We know your presence. We know your love, and that's what we want to pass on to this young people. Help us, God. Save us. We are in need of your hand. Help us encourage, love, support, love, affirm, and love some more. Amen.

14 Swallowed by a Carpet

"Six days you shall labor and do all your work, but the seventh day is a Sabbath to the LORD your God. On it you shall not do any work, neither you, nor your son or daughter, nor your manservant or maidservant, nor your animals, nor the alien within your gates."

—Exodus 20:9-10, NIV

One of my favorite songs is an old Billy Joel tune called "Pressure." The video that went along with the song had one slightly disturbing visual. (Understand that this song came out when artists first discovered that a video could consist of more than putting up one camera that would just film them playing the song.) Joel seems to be slowly sucked down into the carpet, as if his floor suddenly became a shag quicksand. Even those of us who liked the song found the video difficult to watch, because when you watched the video, you couldn't help but think, "Yeah, I can relate to that."

Here's a popular game that is played at many youth meetings: The group is divided into two teams, and each team is given a server's tray. At one end of a large room are several dozen paper cups filled with water. One person from each team runs to the other end of the room and returns with a cup of water on the tray. A second person on each team must do the same, while balancing the first cup as well. This continues with each player on each team retrieving another cup on the tray. Pretty soon the trays are full and players are stacking cups on top of cups. Inevitably someone eventually slips and spills everything, and the team must start over.

One of your parents called your boss at home on Monday, his day off, to tell him about something you said on Sunday night. You just found out that a group of parents are meeting regularly on Tuesday mornings to compare your performance with that of your predecessor. Three of your regular students told you they don't want to come anymore because, "Nobody cool is here anymore." Your lawn needs mowed; your spouse hasn't seen you in a week; the administrative board wants to see your five-year goals; and the bank called to say that someone has stolen your credit card number and charged three thousand dollars worth of "items" from an adult lingerie website.

Tired yet?

There's an important thing to remember here: You're not God. You can't do everything. You have to stop and rest sometimes. Sabbath is important.

Steve Case

Sabbath is vital. Too bad you're usually working on everybody else's day of rest. When do you get time to be alone? When do you get time to pray? When do you get time to be quiet?

Farmers in biblical times actually kept a "sabbath" piece of land. One-seventh of their land was allowed to rest for a season. Nothing was planted on it. It was given time to rest, to rejuvenate. Don't you deserve the same?

You are not a servant of the church. You are not a servant of the Christian education committee. You are not a servant of the senior pastor. You are a servant of God. And you cannot serve God *and* something or someone else. When you burn the candle at both ends, it usually burns twice as fast and then burns out twice as quick.

In 1 Kings 19:11-18 Elijah is standing out on the cliff outside a cave where he has gone to hide from those who are out to get him. God speaks to Elijah on the mountain, but not in fire, earthquake, or a strong wind. God speaks to Elijah in still silence, and the prophet is only able to listen when the fires and the winds and the earthquakes have subsided.

You have permission to unplug the phone. You have permission to sit on the couch and watch old movies and eat ice cream right out of the container. You have permission to drive without listening to the CDs of the lecture at the convention that you didn't get to go to because it was on the senior pastor's Sunday off—the Sunday thus chosen to be "Youth Sunday."

Refill the emptiness in your spirit. Save that one special piece of music that fills your soul during your sabbath time. Don't just take the time off. Make it purposeful. Sleep to rest your body. Be silent to rest your tired ears. Sit on the roof of a building or hill and stare at the stars to rest your tired spirit.

You teach your students that God is a very real presence in their lives. Don't forget that God is a very real presence in yours too.

Prayer: God of the sabbath, give us a sabbath for our souls. Let us rest. Let us think of nothing and hear nothing except the sound of our own breathing. Let us listen for the still, small voice that will pass by us like a breath on the wind. Renew us. Amen.

15 Saul's Tragic Flaw, Our Great Hope

Saul said, "They have brought them from the Amalekites for the people spared the best of the sheep and the cattle, to sacrifice to the LORD your God; but the rest we have utterly destroyed." Then Samuel said to Saul, "Stop! I will tell you what the Lord said to me last night." He replied, "Speak."

Samuel said, "Though you are little in your own eyes, are you not the head of the tribes of Israel? And the LORD sent you on a mission, and said, 'Go, utterly destroy the sinners, the Amalekites, and fight against them until they are consumed.' Why then did you not obey the voice of the LORD? Why did you swoop down on the spoil, and do what was evil in the sight of the LORD?"

—1 Samuel 15:15-19

Poor Saul. He is without question one of the most tragic figures in the often tragic Old Testament. Like any great tragic character from literature, Saul had a fundamental flaw that was his undoing. Saul's flaw was his own distorted self-perception.

When the prophet Samuel told Saul that he would be anointed king—that he would become the king that Israel had demanded of God—Saul took it as good news. But when the time came for the crowning, Saul's feelings had changed. Samuel gathered together the whole nation for what would be (in reality television lingo) "the reveal." Samuel pointed to the tribe from which the king was to be chosen, then the clan, and then the family. Then he had every man in the family parade by him. As Israel waited with baited breath, Samuel had to announce that Israel's new king was not there. (See 1 Samuel 10:17-24.)

Saul was hiding behind a big pile of luggage. He simply couldn't see himself as a king.

Of course, Samuel went ahead and crowned and anointed the new king, but Saul never did get over his feeling of inadequacy. Saul's reign would be marred by failure, missteps, and an inability to obey God in the face of the people's demands. He had everything that a king needed in the ancient world: He was strong and handsome; he stood "head-and-shoulders" above all his peers. But when Saul looked in the mirror, he didn't see a king. So Saul gave

Tony Jones

in to the people's desires and cost himself his throne. We can almost hear the disappointment in Samuel's voice: "Though you were small in your own eyes, God anointed you king!"

Like Saul, many youth workers let arrogance get the best of them. Some youth workers use their position of authority to fill their own twisted needs for importance and power. But youth workers' arrogance, of course, only covers a much more common problem: their feelings of inadequacy. You might experience these feelings as you get up to speak at youth group ("What do I have to say that is of any interest to them?"), as you walk to a coffee shop to meet with a youth ("What in the world am I going to say about her parents' divorce?"), as you drive to the Fall Retreat ("How can these parents entrust their precious children to me for a weekend?"), or as you lie awake in the middle of the night ("Maybe I shouldn't be in ministry ...").

What we forget at these times, however, is that God sees something in us that we can't see in ourselves. God has anointed us youth workers. It's no mistake. So look in the mirror and see what God sees. Really, go look. Right now, look in a mirror.

You see, you're wearing a crown.

Question: What perceived inadequacies are keeping you from living fully into your calling?

Prayer Focus: For God to use you—all of you, inadequacies and all—for the ministry to which you have been called.

16 Two Sides of the Coin

So they watched him and sent spies who pretended to be honest, in order to trap him by what he said, so as to hand him over to the jurisdiction and authority of the governor. So they asked him, "Teacher, we know that you are right in what you say and teach, and you show deference to no one, but teach the way of God in accordance with the truth. Is it lawful for us to pay taxes to the emperor, or not?" But he perceived their craftiness and said to them, "Show me a denarius. Whose head and whose title does it bear?" They said, "The emperor's." He said to them, "Then give to the emperor the things that are the emperor's, and to God the things that are God's." And they were not able in the presence of the people to trap him by what he said; and being amazed by his answer, they became silent.

—Luke 20:20-26

As youth workers, we are asked lots of questions (because adolescents are question-askers). Yes, they'll grow out of it. As teenagers get older, they'll have teachers and friends, pastors and bosses who will make it clear that questions are not OK. They will be told—verbally and non-verbally—that questions are a sign of weakness or are just downright annoying.

But thanks be to God that we get youth at an age when they still have lots of questions. They want to know what God thinks about an issue and what the church's teaching says on that issue. Youth want to know if they should date a certain person and if God has the one already picked out for them. ("And if God knows," they ask themselves, "will God tell me?") They wonder if they should go to college and which college to attend, what profession they should enter, and whether lying to their parents to keep a friend's secret is OK.

Of course, Jesus was often asked questions, by several different people. In the short confrontation about paying taxes, recounted by Matthew, Mark, and Luke (above), Jesus is approached by some Pharisees and some Herodians. Now it's important to know that these two groups did not get along. The Pharisees hated Rome; the Herodians (especially Herod, their leader) had ties to the Roman establishment. Put simply, these groups did not play together nicely on the playground at recess.

But the threat of Jesus was just enough to get these two opposing groups to join forces. They figured that they could trap the Nazarene teacher with this question about taxes. If Jesus said, "Don't pay the tax," the Herodians could have him arrested for insurrection. And if he said, "Go ahead and pay the tax," the Pharisees would ruin his credibility as a Jewish revolutionary. They thought they had him trapped in what philosophers call a "binary opposition." That is, there are just two choices, and no way out.

But Jesus was no ordinary philosopher. He answered his opponents' question with a question (a great tactic, by the way, to use with junior high small groups). The hidden double entendre is that Caesar's image is on the coin, so the coin officially belongs to Caesar, but Caesar himself is created in the image of God, so the coin ultimately belongs to God. Ha! Jesus turned the tables, and his opponents were left with one possible response: silence.

What is most noteworthy here, I think, is how Jesus responded to a trap set up by his adversaries. When those who had chosen to live in community with him asked him questions, he answered, often with beautiful parables that still speak to us today.

We are not required to have all the answers to our youths' questions. But we are required to let youth know that Jesus will answer their questions and that their part is to stay close to him and listen hard.

Challenge: Spend time talking with your students encouraging their questions and reassuring them amid their doubts.

17 Seven Ways

Hear, O Israel: The Lord is our God, the Lord alone. You shall love the Lord your God with all your heart, and with all your soul, and with all your might. Keep these words that I am commanding you today in your heart.

—Deuteronomy 6:4–6

Good communicators know that if they want their audience to remember their message, they must convey the message seven different times in seven different ways. The music minister at my church follows that rule of thumb. She puts articles in the church newspaper, creates her own monthly direct mailing, sends emails to the choir members, makes announcements at rehearsals, lists music ministry events in the local paper, makes reminder phone calls, and sends postcards to publicize upcoming events. Rarely is she disappointed by low turnout or the dreaded whine, "but I didn't know." She gives no one an excuse for forgetting.

Apparently, this rule of thumb goes back a few thousand years. God wants to be sure that the community of faith remember God's commandments and God's covenant with Israel.

Recite them to your children and talk about them when you are at home and when you are away, when you lie down and when you rise. Bind them as a sign on your forehead, and write them on the doorposts of your house and on your gates.

—Deuteronomy 6:7–9

These verses in Deuteronomy explain the first commandment, "You shall have no other gods before me" (Exodus 20:3). God wants Israel to remember this most important commandment, to remind themselves of its importance. So God provides the Israelites seven ways to communicate this commandment to their nation and its individual citizens.

What if we were to put God's word before us in our homes? when we are away? when we lie down and when we rise up? What if we read Scripture for nourishment instead of just to plan a lesson? What if we viewed worship as a chance to renew our relationship with God instead of as an obligation or as part of our jobs? What if we set aside time in the morning and the evening to listen for God instead of bringing a laundry list of personal concerns? How can we—in our lives of professional ministry—recover Scripture as a

Kara Lassen Oliver

reminder of God's covenant and a symbol of God's faithfulness instead of as an object to be "gotten" or a tool of the trade?

Is it possible that, if we kept God's Word ever before us physically—reading it, studying it, posting it in our office—the insights and strength we needed in times of joy and trial would be right before our eyes and upon our hearts? If we found seven different ways to come into contact with Scripture, we might be better equipped in the face of pain and exhaustion; we may not be as likely to forget God's commands and God's love in times of sadness or times of pride. Just as a diploma hanging on the wall reminds us of the time and energy that we have devoted to equipping ourselves for our work in the world, having Scripture visually before us reminds us of our calling and the gifts that equip us for ministry. Just as wearing a wedding ring reminds one that her or his spouse not only loves her or him but also is committed to her or him through whatever life may bring, wearing the symbols of our faith or displaying them in our homes and offices can be a visual reminder of God's faithfulness to us. God wants to be known to us as the only true God, our Creator, and has provided us with the resources to live faithfully. God wants us to be intentional about using those resources and keeping them nearby, so that we remember God's covenant with us.

Not only do we need to communicate in God's name the opportunities that we provide through our ministries, but we also must we allow space and time for God to communicate to us the opportunities for us to better know God. Those who do not pick up the church newspaper and do not read e-mail may miss out on events that could challenge and transform them. Similarly, if we do not pick up the Bible, infuse our environment with symbols of our faith, or attend worship, we may be missing God's offers of love and transformation.

> Prayer: God, you tell us who we are through your Word. Remind us that our souls need the nourishment of your Holy Word. You offer guidance, rest, peace, and hope in the pages of the Bible. Help us to meet you there. Amen.

18 | Heart's Desire

O LORD, you have searched me and known me.
You know when I sit down and when I rise up;
    you discern my thoughts from far away.
You search out my path and my lying down,
    and are acquainted with all my ways.
Even before a word is on my tongue,
    O LORD, you know it completely.
You hem me in, behind and before,
    and lay your hand upon me.
Such knowledge is too wonderful for me;
    it is so high that I cannot attain it.

For it was you who formed my inward parts;
    you knit me together in my mother's womb.
I praise you, for I am fearfully and wonderfully
    made.
    Wonderful are your works;
that I know very well.

—Psalm 139:1-6, 13-14

Youth ministry is many things: spiritual formation, Christian education, mission and outreach, community building, and lots of fun. Of the many jobs that a youth minister performs, the most humbling is the one-on-one relationships with youth and their parents. To be trusted, to be criticized, to be called, and to be rejected is all part of being vulnerable and committing to relationships grounded in Christian love.

Being effective youth ministers—who are compassionate, empower our youth, and recognize their gifts and graces—requires believing in ourselves and recognizing our gifts and graces. If we cannot love ourselves as God loves us, then we cannot love those whom God brings into our ministry as neighbors and companions on the journey.

Anyone who dares to walk as a disciple understands both the strength and vulnerability of the human spirit. Life is difficult and challenging. And in the face of life's challenges we often feel too overwhelmed to consider what God has created us to do and be. Then again, if we are not challenged, we may get too comfortable to seek out our true calling. In addition to life's difficulties and comforts, some of us give up on following God's call because we get impatient. But if we give up listening to God for our true calling, we sacrifice joy in favor of monotony. If we get too impatient and give up, we will likely fill our

Kara Lassen Oliver

schedules with tasks to be accomplished instead of pursuing interests that nurture and develop our unique, God-given gifts. We can carelessly convince ourselves that others—not us—have been called and that we can go ahead with the career of our choosing.

Too many of us doubt our God-given gifts and abilities. Society plays on those doubts, convincing us that being made in the image and likeness of God is not enough to be a complete person. But we trust that being crafted in God's image is enough. Our callings are worth the time it takes to discern and pursue them. But we can only do this if we love ourselves. Then, when we are traveling the path that God has created for us, we can encourage and empower others to do the same.

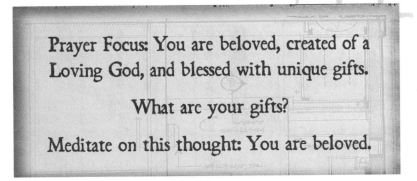

Prayer Focus: You are beloved, created of a Loving God, and blessed with unique gifts.

What are your gifts?

Meditate on this thought: You are beloved.

19 Climbing the Ladder

Just then a lawyer stood up to test Jesus.
"Teacher," he said, "what must I do to inherit
eternal life?" He said to him, "What is written in
the law? What do you read there?" He answered, "You
shall love the Lord your God with all your heart, and with all
your soul, and with all your strength, and with all your mind;
and your neighbor as yourself." And he said to him, "You have
given the right answer; do this, and you will live."

—Luke 10:25-28

As youth ministers, we are entrusted with the caring for and nurturing young people's souls. We point them to God's unconditional love and provide opportunities for them to experience that love. Ideally, when we love teenagers and nurture their spiritual growth, we also nurture our own. Being able and willing to extend ourselves to others is a sign of love and a discipline of faith. When we are confident in God's love and confident in ourselves, we will not burn out or resent our spiritual gifts. Instead, we will mature in our relationship with God and find blessings in our relationships.

Last summer on a high ropes course, I experienced this seeming contradiction of ministering to others by becoming confident in my own gifts. But in this instance I was not extending love, I was receiving. Marie—a lanky, thirteen-year-old girl with seemingly little strength and a one-minute attention span—and I were paired to climb a forty-foot suspension ladder. I made the assumption that I was doing Marie a favor by being her partner. (I like to think of myself as rather strong and athletic; heights do not scare me, and I am competitive by nature.) I naively thought that I could scale this ladder and that I would help take Marie as high as she wanted to go. At the bottom of the ladder, the rungs were about three feet apart. They grew further apart with each rung. Near the top, the rungs were further apart than my five-foot two-inch frame.

Quickly I realized that our ladder-climbing experience would not go as planned. The rope swayed, my helmet kept slipping, and I was unable to jump high enough to get my torso over the rung above me. Marie, on the other hand, could easily jump, shimmy, and climb to each successive rung. Being competitive, and somewhat proud, I was determined to make it at least halfway up the ladder. But I couldn't do it alone. We discovered that if Marie bent her legs, I could stand on her thigh, giving me the extra height I needed to hoist myself up. Then she could nimbly climb up after me. This strategy worked well for a couple rungs. But by the final two rungs I was very frustrated.

Kara Lassen Oliver

I looked at Marie and was ready to give up. But she said firmly, "No. We can make it." She encouraged me, stayed focused on our task, and never gave up. As we scaled that ladder, Marie knew that she had the will and the strength to make it to the top. The most humbling part of the experience for me was that she could have made it to the top a lot easier by herself. But she believed that I also had the strength to do it and wanted me to get to the top with her. She bolstered my will with her words and determination. With Marie providing encouragement and support —literally, as I stood on her leg—I was able to focus intensely on what I needed to do to make it to the top. I did not have to take care of her or worry about her. What a gift! Marie loved herself and was confident in her abilities; and so she was able to help me find the same love and confidence in myself. And together we accomplished a great feat.

That experience changed both of us. Marie showed me that I needed to be aware of my own gifts and abilities, faults and weaknesses and that I needed to love myself. When I recognize those talents and shortcomings in myself and own them, I am freed from needing others' opinions and affirmations to be loving, understanding, and strong. Marie discovered on that ladder that she was, as a child of God, more than people saw her to be. The strength she found in that realization was enough to enable both of us to reach our full potential. When I can be confident in who I am created to be, then I am freed to love others and to help them embrace and celebrate who they are as children of God.

Prayer: Lord, thank you for the Maries in our youth ministries who point us to you when we cannot see beyond ourselves. Forgive us for our pride and open our eyes to see that your strength is sufficient for all of our tasks.
Amen.

20 Fluffy Chicks

One of the scribes came near and heard them disputing with one another, and seeing that he answered them well, he asked them, "Which commandment is the first of all?" Jesus answered, "The first is, 'Hear O Israel: the Lord our God, the Lord is one; you shall love the Lord your God with all your heart, and with all your soul, and with all your mind, and with all your strength.' The second is this, 'You shall love your neighbor as yourself.' There is no other commandment greater than these." Then the scribe said to him, "You are right, Teacher; you have truly said that 'he is one, and besides him there is no other'; and 'to love him with all the heart, and with all the understanding, and with all the strength,' and 'to love one's neighbor as oneself,'—this is much more important than all whole burnt offerings and sacrifices." When Jesus saw that he answered wisely, he said to him, "You are not far from the kingdom of God." After that no one dared to ask him any questions.

—Mark 12:28-34

With each month and week I spend in youth ministry, I become more convinced that loving the youth as best I can is more important that doing and saying the right thing in every situation. I am learning to be more attentive to the meaning behind a youth's words, body language, and silence. But even when I am successfully attentive to every detail, I still am often unsure how to best help a youth, a parent, or a family. A wise man told me recently that, when he isn't sure what is best for an individual, he holds that person in prayer using a specific image from his life that represents God's unconditional love. He imagines that person in his mind's eye safe, secure, and loved. Not being as wise as he, I tried to use his image in my prayers for persons that I was not sure how to love. But using a borrowed image was not effective. I needed an image of my own. While I was at the Heifer Project Ranch on a youth mission trip, God gave me my image.

Each night at the ranch we received a sign-up sheet that listed the next day's learning and service opportunities. One night the last slot on the sheet was for "livestock," so I reported to Jenna (one of the ranch workers) the next morning at 8:30 A.M. for three hours of animal duty. In the pouring rain Taylor and Katie (two of my youth) and I headed to the barn where eighty baby chicks had just been brought up from the field, nearly drowned from the terrible storm the night before. They lay in layers on top of one another in two inch-by-three inch plastic carrying cases. The staff person whom we were helping began stringing heat lamps above a pen; then we quickly grabbed

Kara Lassen Oliver

limp, wet chicks and placed them under the heat lamps. Some laid where we placed them, not moving. Several immediately and instinctively stood and moved to the heat. A few even stood on top of others to get as close to the heat as they could. In a matter of minutes we had moved these pathetic, wet creatures into the pen.

Soon another volunteer arrived with some dry towels and a small hair dryer. Looking into the pens we reached for one chick at a time—my first instinct was to take time looking for the chick that appeared most critical, but I quickly changed my tactic and simply took the ones I could reach most easily. How long could I nurse one before putting it back, still wet, still cold? Would the hair dryer help or burn? Would rubbing them with a towel pull out their young feathers? These were just chicks, but we were making life-or-death decisions for these creatures in our care. The decision to choose one chick over another was arbitrary. And I was surprised how frustrated and burdened I was by that realization.

At the ranch we had so many other animals to care for that we moved the healthiest and most rambunctious chicks to a new pen, put a heater in with the others, and went to milk the goats, feed the rabbits, and herd the cattle who had wandered away in the storm. Before lunch we went back to check on the chicks. The sight we saw was amazing to behold. All but eight of the chicks had survived. Their fluffy down, and not prickly chicken skin, was the first thing I saw. The chicks were no longer lying motionless but up and walking, vying for their turn near the heater or under the lamps. Our seemingly arbitrary and meager efforts had been enough.

Loving them, with heart, soul, mind, and strength had been enough. The spirit of life in Creation is stronger than I had previously given it credit for, and our willingness to participate in God's creation was multiplied that day.

In the same way, the youth entrusted to us do not need our burnt offerings and sacrifices as much as they need us to love them with heart, soul, mind, and strength. We may not always say the right thing, or show up at their school performances, or agree with everything they do. But if we love them, then God will honor our commitments.

Since that day, when I lift persons in prayer, I see them as delicate chicks held softly, but securely, in willing hands—lifted to the warmth of God's love. And I have renewed confidence that the strength of the human spirit in each of us, paired with the love and possibilities in God is enough to bring us through the storms to new life.

Challenge: Find an image to use as you bring your youth before God in prayer.

21 A Time for Everything

[A lawyer] asked Jesus, "And who is my neighbor?" Jesus replied, "A man was going down from Jerusalem to Jericho, and fell into the hands of robbers, who stripped him, beat him, and went away, leaving him half dead. Now by chance a priest was going down that road; and when he saw him, he passed by on the other side. So likewise a Levite, when he came to the place and saw him, passed by on the other side. But a Samaritan while traveling came near him; and when he saw him, he was moved with pity. He went to him and bandaged his wounds, having poured oil and wine on them. Then he put him on his own animal, brought him to an inn and took care of him. The next day he took out two denarii, gave them to the innkeeper, and said, 'Take care of him; and when I come back, I will repay you whatever more you spend.' Which of these three, do you think, was a neighbor to the man who fell into the hands of the robbers?" He said, "The one who showed him mercy." Jesus said to him, "Go and do likewise."

—Luke 10:29-37

As youth ministers we are going all the time—going to the office, going to meetings, going to basketball games, going to performances, going to get coffee. We try very hard to be everything to everyone—staff, parents, volunteers, and youth. Is all this doing and going the way we best love God with all our heart, soul, strength, and mind?

When the lawyer asks Jesus how to inherit eternal life, Jesus turns the question back on the lawyer. And the lawyer answers rightly, citing a commandment memorized by all faithful Jews. Jesus affirms his answer and tells him, "Do this, and you will live." When the lawyer goes one step further, asking Jesus, "Who is my neighbor?" Jesus then tells him the story of the priest, the Levite, and the Samaritan. The point of Jesus' parable is that the one who does something, the one who shows mercy, is truly the neighbor. If we were to stop there, with the parable of the good Samaritan, it would seem that all our doing is indeed the best way to serve God and to love neighbor.

After telling the story, Jesus visits Mary and Martha (Luke 10:38-42). Martha wants Jesus to chastise Mary for sitting at Jesus' feet and listening. Martha is upset that not only does Mary ignore the duties of hospitality, but also that she could be so presumptuous to assume that she can listen and learn like a disciple. But Jesus encourages Martha not to be distracted by "many things" (verse 41). Mary has chosen the "better part" and it will benefit her (verse 42).

Jesus would have us remove whatever distractions in our lives make it difficult to hear God's voice and call. The lawyer needed to go and do. Martha needed to

Kara Lassen Oliver

sit and listen. Our needs are different at different times in our ministry. Knowing exactly what we need is a matter of spiritual discernment. I was struck recently with how negligent I had been to sit and listen:

I woke one morning, rushed around the house to get ready, rushed my daughter to get her ready for school early, made it to church without forgetting anything, dropped off my daughter, got a cup of coffee, walked briskly to my meeting room, and made it to my 9:00 a.m. meeting just a few minutes late. I sat down unprepared for the meeting—no calendar, no Bible, no pen—and yet the meeting was a complete success.

My meeting was a *Companions in Christ* small group. I had debated whether I had the time to commit—whether I could take time away from my job. When I sat down on the couch with nothing but a coffee in hand I was overwhelmed with gratefulness. My only responsibilities for this group were to share my thoughts and pray with my group. When asked to explain why we had come to the group, I answered that I wanted to participate in this experience (thinking in the back of my mind that I could then figure out how to adapt it for youth ministry). As I sat there longer, in the peace and grace of the other members of the group, I realized that I have not been a participant in any type of group, outside of an academic class, since college. I am always responsible, in some way for each Bible Study and small group experience I've been involved with.

All those experiences of being in charge—with youth and with adults—have been rewarding and nourishing for me. I have grown mentally and spiritually through each of them. But just one meeting with my *Companions in Christ* group fed me in a new way—a way that I had forgotten existed. I had a unique opportunity to focus, reflect, and listen deeply for God's call in my life.

We spend a lot of time giving of ourselves—in school, at work, on committees, for family or neighbors. Sitting in that room with my small group and listening, I was overcome with how unhealthy only *giving* of myself had been. I had not, and maybe could not, realize how empty I was until I experienced the Christian nurture and communal care that I have now experienced. My group reminded me that discipleship is a cycle of giving and receiving nurture.

Challenge: Consider where you find yourself in your discipleship. If you need nurture, seek out an available opportunity that will feed and challenge you spiritually. If you have been intentional about nurturing your own soul, pat yourself on the back and look for new ways to go and do, serving God with all your heart, soul, strength, and mind.

22 The Lambs Are Hungry

The third time he said to him, "Simon, son of John, do you love me?"

Peter was hurt because Jesus asked him the third time, "Do you love me?" He said, "Lord, you know all things; you know that I love you."

Jesus said, "Feed my sheep."

—John 21:17, NIV

Though I was born and raised in Buffalo, New York (the "City of Good Neighbors"), I'm a real New Yorker now. That is, I live in New York City—Manhattan, to be exact. I pay too much rent for an apartment that's way too small; I walk fast even when I'm not running late; and I don't speak to folks on the elevator. While I've only lived in New York for about a year, I've learned quickly to fit right into this place known as "The City."

Like many of the other millions crammed into this small corner, I ride the subways. Characteristic of these underground labyrinths are the performers—from tin-pan drummers to violinists to vocalists of all sorts—trying to eke out a living. They have honed their craft, attempting to "wow" you in the ten-second interval you're in their view, as you dart to catch the uptown "A" train or the "4" train to Crown Heights, Brooklyn. And then there are the panhandlers who tread up and down the subway cars, pleading for spare change, each with his or her own unique story: There's the old fellow who was just released from Columbia-Presbyterian Medical Center with no insurance to buy the medications needed to heal his open ulcer and the young widow, disowned by her husband's family, with two children to feed.

From time to time, especially when I've just left worship at my East Harlem congregation, a spirit of benevolence comes upon me, compelling me to spare a five- or ten-dollar bill. But don't catch me on a Wednesday. As I've said, I've learned to be a New Yorker. Sometimes as a person in need passes me by, I pretend to be too captivated by the novel or *Times* article I'm reading to acknowledge the human presence just a couple feet away. Or perhaps it's my mp3 player that has my attention. My cop-out of choice, however, is closing my eyes and dozing off or praying or something—at least until that soul is comfortably past where I am sitting or standing on the train. Whatever the matter, I have found ways to rationalize my reaction without feeling guilty. After all, I give my tithes and offerings. Most often I contribute to some form of second- or third-mile giving. Occasionally, I respond to mail solicitations for social causes. Not to mention that the subway signs instruct me to give to a shelter, and not to the "beggars."

Jay Williams

But the gospel can be unsettling. Too often, we slip into our habits and comforts, and forget that the Christian life is one of enormous responsibility. We compartmentalize our lives so that our faith is here and our good deeds are there. Of course, we acknowledge that we give to the poor because of Jesus' commandments, but too often we fail to recognize that confronting the injustices that we encounter daily is not an "add-on" to our faith.

Simon Peter's failure to be in perpetual relationship with the "least, last, and the lost" is exposed when Jesus questions him about his threefold denial. Three times, Jesus asks, "Do you love me?" and Peter gives the immediate and expected response, "Of course, I love you." After Jesus asks a third time, Peter has the audacity to respond with hurt, though he was the one who has denied Jesus three times! Again, Jesus challenges Peter: If you love me, feed my sheep! The command is not to love one another and take care of those in need because Jesus says so. And it's not an order to do these things because they would be pleasing in God's sight. Rather, the declaration to serve is much more fundamental. Because of a Christian's love for Christ—one's faith in Jesus—she or he is called to a life of service.

Peter sins and denies Jesus, but Jesus forgives and reconciles Peter unto him by commanding the troubled disciple to love mercy and seek justice. In other words, service is not simply a product of faith, but it is a source of faith. Jesus suggests that it is one thing to ignore him, but something altogether different (and perhaps even more egregious?) to ignore his people. Jesus says clearly that forgiveness is contingent: It is not only God's gift, but also it is God's challenge. While we cannot purchase Christ's love, we do owe something—love and care for neighbor.

So what is the Scripture saying about our everyday living? To give to every passerby, every peddler in the subway? I reckon that the Scripture's message is not that simple. But consider what this world might be if we all freely gave of ourselves. Jesus' message to Peter seems to say that we must live out our faith more deeply than by simply participating in holiday food and clothing drives. We must take our understanding of service beyond our annual youth mission trip or day of volunteering at the homeless shelter. The money and resources we control are a sacred trust—placed in our possession not solely for our own sake, but also for the sake of others and indeed the world. "If you love me, feed my sheep" speaks plainly to the three-party relationship that defines the Christian faith. Holistic faith embodies an inward-upward-outward relationship between self ("you"), God ("me"), and community ("my sheep").

Prayer Focus: For those in need and those capable of helping.

23 Dance Fever

Praise God in his sanctuary; ...
praise him with tambourine and dancing,
praise him with the strings and flute, ...
Let everything that has breath praise the LORD.

—Psalm 150:1b, 4, 6a, NIV

Everybody loves a good party. A familiar biblical story suggests that even Jesus liked to have a good time: He turned water into wine at a wedding celebration, didn't he? (See John 2:1-11). In the Old Testament, because God fulfilled God's promises, King David dances so mightily that his clothes fall off. David's wife, Michal, rebukes him for this seemingly indecent display. But David says to her, "I will celebrate before the Lord. I will become even more undignified than this" (2 Samuel 6:21b-22a). Because of what the Lord has done, David dances, and when his wife tries to get in the way of his praise, he says (in so many words), "If you think that was something, you ain't seen nothing yet!" Then, why in the world are we not having as much fun as David? What has happened that the church has lost its joy? How will the church reclaim its proud witness of praise?

The parable of the prodigal son (Luke 15:11-32), at its core, is about partying. Sure, love, confession, forgiveness, reconciliation, and grace are also themes, but you can't help but notice the emphasis the text places on enjoying oneself. This story looks at celebration and having fun from two perspectives: On the one hand, the younger son wastes his inheritance through "wild living." On the other hand, when the son comes to his senses and returns home, his father spares no expense in celebrating. Luke tells us that there is music and dancing, friends and fine food, and that the guest of honor comes dressed to impress. The parable ends, though, with a bitter older brother, whining because the party is not for him. The brother's jealousy gets in the way of his participation in the festivities. The older brother's attitude begs to question: what gets in the way of our praise?

The prodigal son very easily is any young person who leaves home to go to college, pursue a job, or otherwise "find" herself or himself. The text gives no indication that the son intentionally sets out to squander his inheritance; it is quite possible that he simply wants independence so that he can see the world. But, as we all do, he slips up, loses sight of what is important to him, and makes bad decisions. If our youth are the younger son in the parable, we, as youth workers, can be either the father or the older brother. Either we can prepare the feast, or we can allow things in our life to keep us from going to the party.

Jay Williams

As youth ministers—whether clergy or laity—we are blessed with opportunities to nurture young people in their spiritual journey. Many of these youth have only just begun the journey, and all are learning how to develop a deeper, fuller relationship with Jesus. The guidance we give will have a profound impact on the lives of everyone involved in this ministry, and by implication, all those who are touched by it. In youth ministry, the adult workers are shepherds; the youth are the flocks. Unfortunately, the "stuff" that clutters our lives and hinders our celebration profoundly affects this community. A student, it is said, is only as wise as her or his teacher. Therefore, when we allow conditions and circumstances to interfere with our worship, we not only fail to honor God, but we disrupt the faith journeys of those who look toward us for guidance. Surely the father in the parable is disappointed that his firstborn does not share in the elation. Even so, the father says that celebrating his lost son's return is OK.

And it is right for us to celebrate, no matter what might tempt us to do otherwise. The cause for the party in Jesus' parable is the homecoming of the son—the young person in our church. I believe that youth are the catalysts that will enable the church to grasp again its passion for the gospel. Simply put: vibrant youth ministry will help the church find what it has lost. Because the prodigal son comes to his senses and turns again to the love of his family, the father again praises him. So too might our congregations again be joyful when they welcome unconditionally our young people.

> Prayer Focus: Let our prayer be that the church might dance so passionately that its "clothes"—those things that separate us from our true nature as creatures created in God's image—might fall off.

Greater Expectations

> From everyone who has been given much, much will
> be demanded; and from the one who has been
> entrusted with much, much more will be asked.
>
> —Luke 12:48, NIV

We all used to love the teachers who graded easily. We didn't have to do all the reading to get a good grade, and much of the time we didn't even have to pay attention. In college we called these courses "guts" because all the real work had been removed. One of my teachers, Mr. Fran, however, missed the day in teachers' school when they taught how to be liked by students. Although he was "only" my physical education instructor and basketball coach, his was one class that wasn't to be taken lightly. He was notorious for not allowing absences, whatever the reason. His rule was simple: You miss practice, you don't play in the next game. And if you were caught ditching his class—forget about it!

Mr. Fran did not hesitate to expose his more lenient colleagues, telling me that my other teachers were not doing me a favor by permitting me to submit papers late. In fact, he argued that these instructors were doing me a disservice. In retrospect I realize (as maturing persons often do) that Mr. Fran was correct. Taking the low road does not prepare us for the challenges that inevitably lie ahead. But beyond that Mr. Fran was right to make his players hold fast to their commitments. It *should* be difficult to renege on things to which we commit ourselves—even if it's a voluntary basketball practice.

Why should we, as adults who work with youth, act any differently? We have been entrusted with the awesome responsibility of nurturing the faith development of young Christians. No doubt, this ministry is a gift from God and a calling. But it is also a burden—a responsibility—that must not be taken lightly. Parents depend upon teachers to play a lead role in their child's education; so do they depend upon us to play a lead role in their child's spiritual growth. Our task is to help youth discover their gifts and passions, to learn how to navigate through difficult choices, and to become strong leaders.

In our society "getting by" has become all too easy. Far too often we are willing to reduce everything to the lowest common denominator. We are creatures of habit with deadened senses who have grown accustomed to the way things are. Complacency is rewarded by our culture: Don't rock the boat, don't fall out of step, and you are sure to be well liked by those in positions of influence and authority. At times even our churches have become predictable institutions, willing to accept anything that is normal or traditional or easy and unwilling to change. While we expect God to work miracles in our lives, we do

Jay Williams

not demand the same of ourselves. The status quo, however, is the last thing that Christ's example teaches us to do.

Youth ministry at its core is about preparing world-changing young disciples. It is about developing leaders, for the future, but also for the present. How many times have we heard the frustrating comment that "youth are the church of tomorrow"? Could it be that we are making this claim a reality by not requiring the best from our young people right here, right now? We must set the bar higher day after day, constantly challenging our youth to do more and be more. When we fail to do so, we fail our young people. The times in which we live require Christians who are bold in love and humble in service. Perhaps the improvement in our communities we all desire begins in our very own youth ministries. "Be the change you want to see," it has been said. Paul exhorts such a high calling in Philippians 3:14 (NIV): "I press on toward the goal to win the prize for which God has called me heavenward in Christ Jesus." Mediocrity is unacceptable. Taking whatever we can get— from our youth or ourselves—is not acceptable. Should we be more specific here? Living out the fullness of our potential must be the bare minimum. Why should we demand anything less than excellence?

As youth workers, we are typically overworked and under-appreciated. Most people do not understand the incredible care and commitment—the devotion—that this ministry requires. Similarly, devotional living is no easy task. It is not simply reading a story, reciting a Scripture, and mouthing a prayer. If we use devotion simply as a tool to keep our motors running, we miss the point. From time to time, we have to stop, look under the hood, and fix what is wrong. Devotional living, like youth ministry, is a commitment. It is a deeply introspective process that requires us to look carefully at ourselves and our ministries, honestly examining where we succeed and where we fail. We must ask the tough questions, like, Are we really challenging our young people? and in turn, Are we challenging ourselves?

Never was it said that responding to God's call to youth ministry would be easy. In fact Christ said it plainly: "Anyone who does not carry his cross and follow me cannot be my disciple" (Luke 14:27, NIV). He also assured us, saying, "Rejoice and be glad, because great is your reward in heaven" (Matthew 5:12, NIV). And when the young people in our youth groups live out their potential, in no small part to the guidance we have provided, we get to sample this reward on earth.

Prayer Focus: For the courage to require more of your youth and youth ministry.

25 It's All in the Hands

> I sent him this reply: "Nothing like what you are
> saying is happening; you are just making it up out
> of your head."
> They were all trying to frighten us, thinking, "Their hands
> will get too weak for the work, and it will not be completed."
> But I prayed, "Now strengthen my hands."
>
> —Nehemiah 6:8-9, NIV

When was the last time you worked with your hands? Certainly, we use our hands all the time, but not in the same way that Nehemiah did. He was rebuilding a wall that God had called him to complete. In fact, Nehemiah was on a leave of absence from working for King Artaxerxes. Nehemiah was so visibly saddened when he heard news from Jerusalem saying that the wall had been destroyed and its gates burned that the king granted him leave. (See Nehemiah 1 for the full story.)

Nehemiah ends up in Jerusalem with the king's blessing and meets obstacles at every turn. Every one of us knows how that feels. God calls us to do something—take a certain job, attend a class, reach out to a student, step out in faith—and we respond with obedience and trust. We are so excited because we know that God has called us, God has equipped us, and God is walking with us. Smug and secure, we think that we have everything under control—until the roadblocks emerge. Whether a lack of financial backing for a mission trip or a shortage of volunteers for a youth group event or some other unforeseen barrier, we feel especially frustrated because we were supposed to have been working on God's project. God called us! We throw our hands in the air, outraged at God's apparent absence at the time of our greatest need.

Nehemiah, too, must have experienced that same frustration. As he attempted to rebuild the wall, he faced opposition from all sides. First his enemies mocked him and criticized his workmanship. When their jeers failed to delay Nehemiah, his adversaries began to attack his workers. Before long, Nehemiah's friends were starting to doubt. They began arguing amongst themselves. When Nehemiah finally resolved the morale issue, the trouble began in earnest! Nehemiah was questioned, belittled, and maligned—some even plot to kill him.

But instead of throwing his hands in the air and quitting, Nehemiah placed his hands before God and asked for strength—strength to complete the task, strength to do what needed to be done without complaint or fatigue. Then, incredibly, he placed his enemies in God's hands and asked God to treat them justly.

Lynne Wells Graziano

And the wall? Nehemiah completed the wall in fifty-two days, assured that he had God's support. What task in your life today requires the strength that comes from God?

Challenge: Pick a task this week using your hands—whether typing, washing dishes, or building a wall—and let God's strength show through the work of your hands.

> Prayer: God of strength and mercy, strengthen my hands today. Let them work without distraction or defeat at the tasks you have set before me.

26   Remember ... I Am

Remember the former things, those of long ago;
I am God and there is no other;
I am God, and there is none like me.

—Isaiah 46:9, NIV

If you are like me, you often find yourself making lists in your mind instead of focusing on the tasks in front of you. So clear your head right now. Before you read this devotion, take a few moments to jot down everything you need to remember today, or this week.

Ready? Because God has a memo for us: Isaiah 46:9. Read it again. While you have your Bible open, go back and read verse 8 as well, "Remember this, fix it in mind, take it to heart, you rebels." Rebels? Us? Could God really be calling us rebels—surely this verse is just a reference to those naughty Israelites in Isaiah's time—right?

Sorry, friends, but I think God is talking to each one of us through this Scripture. The Lord of Creation knows our rebellious nature. God knows our desire to serve ourselves and forget about our Creator, when it's convenient. We may not have been enslaved by the Egyptians, wandered in the desert for forty years, or faced battles as intense as those recorded in the Old Testament, but we probably have been enslaved by money, or ambition, or idolatry. Our wanderings, though less eventful, have been equally hurtful to God. So the message to us is worth repeating: "I am God, and there is no other; I am God, and there is none like me."

Remember? God's message is far more important than whatever we jotted down on our "to do" list. God is reminding us that history is God's story written for us so that we can remember the former things: Creation, sin, covenants, and commandments; Adam, Eve, Noah, Moses, David, Esther, Isaiah .... God's story tells the life stories of rulers and slaves, righteous heroes and evil kings, faithful followers and wicked rebels. Which passage from God's Word did you put on your list to read this week?

What? You forgot to write down what part of the Bible you want to study this week? Perhaps you didn't write anything down because you always remember where you are reading and what you are studying. Scripture time probably is so firmly entrenched in your routine that it falls in the same category as brushing your teeth, taking showers, and filling your car with gasoline—you don't need to write it down because you never forget. I applaud your dedication, because I'm more like the rebels God addresses in Isaiah 46. I need to write down my weekly Scripture readings to help "fix it in mind" and "take it to heart" (Isaiah 46:8).

Lynne Wells Graziano

Go back to your list of all the things you want to remember today or this week. Add, "Read Isaiah 46." Then add another selection from the Bible you haven't read in a while, or the name of a person in the Bible you remember from Sunday school whose story you can't recall. If you aren't already a "regular"—if Scripture reading is not on your daily "to do" list—and eagerly anticipate each encounter with the great I AM, make reading and studying the Bible part of your routine. God waits to meet you there.

Challenge: Prioritize daily time with God and write down what you are learning so that you, rebel or not, will fix God's Word in mind and take it to heart.

Prayer: God without equal, let me shape my life in harmony with your plan, as I read your Word and remember. Amen.

27　Food for Forever

Be careful to follow every command I am giving
you today, so that you may live and increase and
may enter and possess the land that the LORD
promised on oath to your forefathers. Remember how the
LORD your God led you all the way in the desert these forty
years; to humble you and to test you in order to know what was
in your heart, whether or not you would keep his commands. He
humbled you, causing you to hunger and then feeding you with
manna, which neither you nor your fathers had known, to teach
you that man does not live on bread alone but on every word
that comes from the mouth of the LORD.

—Deuteronomy 8:1-3, NIV

Forty years wandering in the desert! Even at forty years old, I have trouble picturing forty years spent in a vast, open desert, griping about the food and accommodations while wondering if I'd ever see the Promised Land. Yet in my own forty years I have spent much time wandering in the desert with overwhelming feelings of emptiness and frustration, of inadequacy and doubt.

In fact, I'd guess most of you have spent time in the desert as well. Sure, some of you might only have wandered in and out for twenty or thirty years, while some of you are veteran wanderers with fifty or more years of desert experiences. Think back to one of those times.

Perhaps you've found yourself in the desert after a "mountaintop moment." You introduced a new youth group member to the Christ you love and serve. You shared the tears of joy and the excitement of that young person experiencing a new birth and recognizing her place in the Body of Christ. You thought, "Finally, I am beginning to see the results of my labor."

Then the bottom fell out. That same excited believer is arrested for possession of illegal drugs. The parents who had thanked you for including their child now want to know "What are you teaching these kids?" and "Why did this happen to my child?" And you start to doubt. Stinging desert sand swirls in your face; the hot wind of disappointment and discouragement rocks you back and forth as you look around for a friend, for encouragement, for relief for your thirsty spirit and aching heart.

Or you might have wandered into the desert over a broken relationship—a parent's rejection, a friend's betrayal, a spouse's infidelity. Blindly you ran into the desert, feeling hurt, angry, and absolutely alone. How long did you wander until you met Jesus there? Was it days? weeks? months? a year or more?

Lynne Wells Graziano

You did meet him there, didn't you? I hope you didn't miss that part of the wandering experience! Matthew 4:1-11 tells us how Jesus was led by the Spirit into the desert wilderness. He wasn't driven by despair or forced there by frustration—he was led by the Spirit. For forty days and forty nights he fasted and, we are told (in one of the greatest understatements of all time) that he was hungry. But does Jesus act on the devil's suggestion to turn the stones to bread? Does he snap his fingers and create an all-you-can eat buffet of divine proportions? No.

I picture Jesus literally getting in the devil's face, looking him in the eye, and saying, "It is written: 'Man does not live on bread alone, but on every word that comes from the mouth of God' " (Matthew 4:4, NIV, quoting Deuteronomy 8:3). One of the lessons borne of forty years of desert wandering is articulated by a hungry, tired Jesus after forty days of fasting in the wilderness: The most important food lasts forever: the Word of God.

Challenge: Find a morsel of God's Word, memorize it and let it quench the thirst in your heart this week.

Prayer: Dear Lord, I pray that, even when I am "full," I will hunger for your Word.

28 It's Not About Me

> For even Christ did not please himself but, as it
> is written: "The insults of those who insult you
> have fallen on me." For everything that was written
> in the past was written to teach us, so that through
> endurance and the encouragement of the Scriptures we might
> have hope.
>
> May the God who gives endurance and encouragement give you
> a spirit of unity among yourselves as you follow Christ Jesus,
> so that with one heart and mouth you may glorify the God and
> Father of our Lord Jesus Christ.
>
> —Romans 15:3-6, NIV

Admit it: Some verses of Scripture are harder to read than others. We read, "You shall not murder" (Exodus 20:13) and think, "That's right, I'm following that rule!" Or we come across, "You are the light of the world. A city on a hill cannot be hid" (Matthew 5:14) and we puff up, knowing that our light is shining bright! But the Scripture above is more difficult. Paul tells us that even Christ "did not please himself." Wait a minute. Does God really expect us not to be looking out for our own interests? We're supposed to pick unity over self?

Maybe you're better at this type of thing than I am, but I struggle with verses like this. Generally, I don't take criticism well; preparing my personal defense often takes precedence over glorifying God. To see Jesus beside me, taking the insults for me, I have to move my eyes off me! Isn't "it" supposed to be about me?

Of course not. And as youth workers, most of us have taught this lesson to our youth numerous times. We've done lessons on the Body of Christ, each person having a part, and God having a plan and purpose for every member of the body. We've asked youth to replace selfishness with selflessness. We teach this lesson so well, but at the same time we forget that we need to learn what God wants to teach us. And we forget to let our youth know that we, too, seek truth in Scripture and struggle to learn, just as they struggle.

I remember one day driving a minivan packed with teenage girls to school following our early morning Bible study. We had been joking about the phrase, "It's all about me." They admitted struggling with "it" not being about them! And I confessed that my prayer group, my Bible study group, my peers and yes, their parents, all struggle to take our eyes off ourselves and keep them focused on God. In unison, they said, "Really?"

Lynne Wells Graziano

You see, youth often think that their parents, leaders, and pastors instinctively have mastered all of God's commands. They think that we have "it" all figured out. Yet they are comforted to know that we too stumble along the way.

Now I'm not saying that parents and youth leaders should go out and confess everything. Youth don't need to know every minute and potentially sordid detail of our struggles. But they do need to know that we struggle at times, and that, when we do, we follow Paul's advice and seek "the encouragement of the Scriptures" to bring us hope. While reminding our youth that we are human is important, it is also essential to point them toward the divine.

Challenge: When you feel the need to make "it" about you, symbolically hand over the situation to Jesus. Then, find endurance and encouragement in Scripture.

Prayer: Lord of unity and strength, show me the way to unite your people, even when it might cost me my "right" to a witty retort or sarcastic answer. Instead, let those who insult me know you and your glory. Amen

29 Body for Life ... Eternal

For physical training is of some value, but
godliness has value for all things, holding
promise for both the present life and the life to
come.

—1 Timothy 4:8, NIV

Do you have the Bowflex® body? If not, you surely know how to get one. You've certainly seen the ads in the paper or on television or heard them on the radio. Getting a well-conditioned athlete's body is so simple: twenty minutes a day, three days a week. "Yeah, right," you've probably said.

Have you seen ads that tell you how to become godly? Probably not. Godliness doesn't seem to be a mainstream goal, at least not where I'm living! And even if the ads ran regularly, how much time do you think it would take "become" godly? I'm pretty sure it would be more than an hour each week.

Yet I know that during the average week I put more effort into exercising and eating right than training for godliness. My earthly body, even though it is a temple for the Holy Spirit, will not go on indefinitely. Paul's first letter to Timothy tells us that godliness has a value beyond this earth, "holding promise for both the present life and the life to come."

I can hear the devoted couch dwellers out there saying, "That's what I'm talking about! I don't need to worry about this earthly body." Sorry, coming up with reasons not to take care of one's body is not the point here. God calls each of us to care for the body we have been given, imperfections and all. Likewise, the physical fitness nut and the buff-body wannabe need to step back and say, "I could afford to schedule some godliness workouts." No matter our level of physical fitness, we could all benefit from practicing our faith.

So where should we start? Just as exercise experts always instruct individuals to see their doctors before beginning a workout regimen, God wants us to visit a heavenly doctor as we intensify our spiritual exercise plan. We can visit the Lord in prayer as we establish our training program. We can check the godly fitness manual, the Holy Bible, for instructions and guidance. And we can find a workout buddy or two—that is, spiritual friends who are perhaps more experienced and willing to share their knowledge by instructing us patiently.

Another important aspect of "godliness training" is establishing goals to measure our progress, just as runners keep mileage logs while training for a set distance. We should ask ourselves, "How will I know that I've become more godly?" Will improved spiritual fitness be reflected in healed relationships,

Lynne Wells Graziano

using less negative or derogatory words, improved mental outlook, or even better ministry results? If we honestly evaluate how we are less than "buff" spiritually, you can begin to work on those "muscles" specifically: muscles of servitude, prayer, unconditional love, Scripture reading, and so on.

Most of all, don't forget to keep going back for check-ups—spiritual exams with the Great Physician. These doctor visits are a prescription good for life eternal.

Challenge: Set one specific "spiritual fitness" goal for this week, and ask a friend to check up on your progress later in the week.

Prayer: Gracious God, giver of life, let me care for my spiritual body with greater effort than I devote to my physical body. Help me improve my life on earth and in the world to come.

30 !¢$%@* You!

> [Elisha] went up from there to Bethel; and while he was going up on the way, some small boys came out of the city and jeered at him, saying, "Go away, baldhead! Go away, baldhead!" When he turned around and saw them, he cursed them in the name of the Lord. Then two she-bears came out of the woods and mauled forty-two of the boys.
>
> —2 Kings 2:23-24

My favorite time to read this passage to my youth group is when they make fun of my clothes, my choice of music, or my latest haircut. For some reason, though, it doesn't scare them; maybe if I actually shave my head ....

The honest truth is that sometimes I wish I had the ability to command a couple of she-bears to maul some folks—sometimes a middle school boy or two, sometimes a parent of one of my kids, sometimes another staff member, and even more often someone on the church board. And I haven't even mentioned people outside the church!

The last time I was driving the church van, some guy pulled out in front of me and slammed on his brakes. The only reason something very un-Christlike didn't escape my lips was that some younger teenagers were there who would've told on me. I wanted to cuss; I really did. Then again, I guess I wanted to curse.

The truth of the matter is that a curse is pretty powerful. Just think of some of the worst cuss words you know; most of them have curses at their roots. We may not literally mean to call down a curse upon someone, but the damage our tongues can do is very real nonetheless.

Jesus cursed a fig tree on his way to Jerusalem because it didn't have any fruit—and figs weren't even in season. The disciples were blown away when they saw the tree later and realized that it would never bear fruit again. In the Scripture above Elisha curses forty-two kids—to death!—because they make fun of his bald head!

James reminds us that everything that comes from our mouths should be for the building up of others, not for their destruction. As Christians, we are called to bless, not to curse. And blessings are just as powerful—in fact, even more so.

We need to be careful about how we speak to the kids in our charge, their parents, the staff, and the church board. As youth workers, we're going to get our share of people who are unhappy with us. And, especially when we are

Will Penner

tired or angry, our verbiage can become abrasive, even hateful. But when we wage war on others within our fellowships, we fail to do the ministry God has called us to. Destruction is always easier than construction, but Christians are called to build up and not tear down one another.

Challenge: As a spiritual discipline, every time you find yourself mentally cursing someone, immediately follow up the curse with a mental blessing. For an even deeper challenge, say aloud the name of the first person who jumped into your mind as you read this devotional. For the next twenty-one days, at least twice each day, pray earnestly for God to abundantly bless that person. And as you encounter him or her, actively seek ways that you can be a blessing, rather than a curse, in his or her life.

Prayer: God, I offer _____ to you, asking you to bless (him or her). Help me recognize that (he or she) is your precious child, and you love (him or her) very much. Change my heart, so that I may no longer be a curse to your children, but a blessing.
In Jesus' name, amen.

37 Gathering the Cloud

Now faith is the assurance of things hoped for,
the conviction of things not seen. Indeed by faith
our ancestors received approval....
Therefore since we are surrounded by so great a
cloud of witnesses, let us also lay aside every weight and run
with perseverance the race that is set before us.

—Hebrews 11:1-2; 12:1

"Youth workers are, in many ways, the incarnation of Christ with kids." "The Holy Spirit resides within us, and for some kids we encounter, our lives may be the only Bible they ever read."

These were the mantras preached to me as a young youth worker, and to some degree they are true. We do, in fact, represent the Holy to our kids. Certainly, they listen to what we teach them about God, and to some degree our theological lenses become their lenses too. This thought, I hope, scares all of us just a bit. I also hope it encourages us to continue to broaden and deepen our own theological reflection and study.

What we teach our youth is very important and can influence their lives in profound ways. Even more powerful than what we teach, though, is what we do. If we treat kids with love and respect, they are more likely to believe that God loves and respects them too. If we are aloof and distant, they may believe that God acts the same way.

Showing God's love through our actions does not, however, mean putting the spotlight on ourselves. If we hog center stage in our youth ministry, then the picture of Christ that we portray will be skewed. Regardless of how well we may reflect Christ's love to youth, if we seek to be the only ones in their lives who are listening to them, discipling them, correcting them, and loving them, then their picture of God is incomplete.

The Bible describes the church as the Body of Christ. It's not accidental that this metaphor insists upon multiple parts in that body. Paul mentions some of those individual parts by name to make this point. He lets us know that the hand's function is much different from the foot's function, and that we need each to do its job for the body to function properly.

In many cases youth workers seek not only to be a different body part than the one we're assigned but also to be multiple parts at once. Often, the more roles we can take, the more our constituents and supervisors praise us. We add to the external pressure with internal pressures of our own, thinking, "If I'm not available to meet all of these kids' needs, who will?"

At best, this is a burnout situation waiting to happen. At worst, it's idolatrous. Paul uses as a metaphor the Body of Christ, not the body of the youth pastor. We are not meant to be all things to all kids, parents, and church board members. And if we're not actively connecting kids to other members of the Body of Christ, we're at best giving them an incomplete representation of Jesus and at worst trying to take the place of Jesus in their lives.

The Scripture above from Hebrews, when applied to youth ministry, encourages us to surround our kids with witnesses who have come before us—those whose stories have been canonized in Scripture or passed down by the traditions of the church. But these verses should also encourage us to actively seek to surround our kids with the witnesses who are in their midst now. Your church or ministry, and indeed the larger community, is full of people who are living, breathing examples of faith, hope, love, hospitality, generosity, and godly living. Our kids' understandings of Christ will become much stronger when they get to see more than just one body part.

Our culture is becoming progressively more interested in individual experience than in the collective understanding of those who have come before. That doesn't give us license to scrimp on teaching Scripture to kids, but it does mean that we can't stop there if we really want to be effective. We also need to point kids toward others who are journeying in the way of Christ.

Challenge: Contact a group of senior adults in your congregation. Ask each senior to invite a youth to join them at their next event. Or invite the parents and siblings to come to the next youth event. (And invite them directly; don't assume that teenagers will do the inviting.)

Prayer: God, it is no mistake that you have surrounded our students with the people in this place. Help me not try to be all parts of the Body by myself. Bring to mind for me those who can do what I cannot, and give me the courage to surround my youth group with a more complete representation of you. In Jesus' name, amen.

32) I Want You!

"I do not call you servants any longer, because the servant does not know what the master is doing; but I have called you friends, because I have made known to you everything that I have heard from my Father. You did not choose me but I chose you. And I appointed you to go and bear fruit, fruit that will last, so that the Father will give you whatever you ask him in my name."

—John 15:15-16

The day after I got my first public school teaching job, the principal told me that he was glad to have chosen such a bright and capable teacher. (He hadn't even seen me teach yet, by the way.) He then told me to let him know if he could serve me in any way. And I was ruined from then on.

In my first youth ministry position, I was blessed to work for a senior pastor who allowed me to grow in ways unheard of in many churches. While offering me his wisdom and experience, he didn't condescend to me or try to fit me into his mold. He allowed me freedom and flexibility to learn and grow in my role as a youth worker. He encouraged me to be creative and experiment rather than do things the way I (and he) had always done them. And he, like my principal, was explicit about serving me in my role.

I think Jesus smiled on both of those bosses, because I was their employee, yet they actively pursued ways to serve me. They could've chosen to use their positions to lord over me, but they chose to follow Jesus' example in their leadership.

In Jesus' time, like today, many who aspire to leadership positions do so in order to control others—or at least influence others. A desire to change others (dare I say manipulate others?) without taking on a servant mentality is not Christlike, regardless of how noble our intentions.

Frankly, Jesus' model is strange, especially when we grow up surrounded by hierarchies. But these hierarchies aren't new. They were also part of the culture two thousand years ago.

In the first century disciples traditionally chose the rabbi they wanted to work with in the same way that a student today might choose a university to attend. The student seeks the university's approval of her or his scholarship ability, applies, and waits for the university to accept or deny her or his application.

But athletic directors often approach outstanding football players, drama departments go after budding young actors, and academic deans seek students

Will Penner

with incredibly high GPAs. They offer tuition reductions, extra perks, or even full-ride scholarships to these students because of what they can bring to the institutions. Similarly, Jesus tells his disciples that he chose them, not the other way around.

We all want kids to feel welcome in our ministries. We work hard to create programs and events that will make them seek us out. But what would our youth ministries look like if our students felt like it wasn't them who chose us, but us who chose them?

Perhaps even more poignant for us is how we "recruit" our volunteer adults. We often make blanket announcements from the pulpit and write bulletin announcements and newsletter articles asking people to let us know if they would like to work with the young people. How might they respond if we choose them instead of asking them to choose us?

How might our young people's (and adult leaders') images of God change if they were to feel "chosen" by us?

Jesus was skilled at turning the rules upside-down. Instead of establishing traditional master-servant relationships with his disciples, he became their servant leader. He tells his disciples that they are his friends, elevating them to a status of equals, which is exactly how we are called to treat our disciples in our youth groups—as co-travelers in the way of Christ. Let's stop hoping kids and adults will knock on our doors; instead, let's reach out and call them by name.

Challenge: Pray about every single adult in the church. Then literally call a few of them and invite them to follow Christ by accompanying the youth. Consider the way you typically invite kids to "your stuff." How might Jesus invite these youth if he were in your particular situation? Share what you're learning with other adults so that they can specifically choose young people whom you might miss.

33 Reliance ... Well, Sorta

> I rejoice in the Lord greatly that now at last
> you have revived your concern for me; indeed, you
> were concerned for me, but had no opportunity to
> show it. Not that I am referring to being in need; for
> I have learned to be content with whatever I have. I know what
> it is to have little, and I know what it is to have plenty. In
> any and all circumstances I have learned the secret of being
> well fed and of going hungry, of having plenty and of being in
> need. I can do all things through him who strengthens me.
>
> —Philippians 4:10–13

Truthfully, this Scripture is pretty much just lip service for most of us. We live very few moments of our day-to-day lives in total dependence upon God. When we're hungry, we don't have to hunt for food—except in the fridge or grocery store aisle. As a result, we're not sure how to be "content in all circumstances."

Instead of being in tune with the constantly changing weather conditions and preparing for our everyday survival, we simply adjust our thermostats, add an extra layer of clothing, or bring an umbrella. Instead of relying upon the goodness of those with whom we share our ministries, we sign contracts guaranteeing our salaries, medical benefits, and retirement accounts.

Instead of spending time in solitude in the wilderness before attending to the needs of our flock, we consult "teacher-proof" curriculum, attend seminars, or purchase the latest book of attention-grabbers for teenagers. Instead of discerning how God is *already* at work in our specific context, we turn to models of youth ministry created by colleagues down the street or across the country and try to recreate their experience in our situation.

When all of our needs are being met, it's easy for us to say that we rely on God when we don't really have to. This is one reason why we are so drawn to people who are in desperate need, who are truly relying on God: the missionary who continues to inoculate children in a third world country despite almost daily death threats; the urban youth worker who continues to minister to gang members despite having no building, no budget, and no help; the young widow with three children who's more active in the church than most married couples; the old man who loses his entire farm in the tornado, yet who still sings gospel songs every Sunday at the top of his lungs.

We must always do three things in times of abundance if we are to make reliance upon God something more than a trite cliché. First, we must make sure to re-awaken our sense of awe and wonder at God's blessings. When it's cold outside and we have a warm bed to sleep in, we can transform an otherwise

Will Penner

hedonistic experience into holy worship by recognizing this comfort as God's gift. When a youth comes to a Bible study, we can be awed and humbled that we are stewards of her or his time, mind, and soul for that hour—instead of dwelling on why three other youth aren't there.

The second thing we can do is to share what we have with others. Saying a blessing prayer over our food and acknowledging others' hunger is not enough. Jesus was very specific in Matthew 25:40. He did not say, "If you thought about the least of these, you thought about me." He also didn't say, "If you did it unto the least of these who were worthy . . . ." Jesus is pretty clear about this in both his words and his actions.

The third thing is to help others see God's hand at work. If we give a dynamic talk and the youth are talking about what a great job we did, instead of what God is calling them to do, we've missed the boat. When we deliver the Christmas baskets and someone tells us how great our church is, if we don't point to Jesus, then we're simply social workers. In the same way that we need to continually remind ourselves that it's God and not the personnel committee who is keeping our light bills paid, we need to point others toward God as the provider of all we have and are able to do. We are simply the couriers.

It's easy for us to say that we trust Christ—until we have no other choice. A constant reminder to ourselves and others (in times of abundance or generosity) that all blessings come from God will help carry us through those times when our source of sustenance (whether physical, social, emotional, or spiritual) is not readily apparent.

Challenge: Make a gratitude list and refer to it often to remind yourself of the ninety-nine percent of life that is going beautifully. Take a homeless man to lunch and simply listen to his story without trying to fix him. Find a way to redirect to God all the praise you receive.

Prayer: Giver of all life, of all love, of all hope, illuminate a few of those blessings that we've taken for granted, and allow gratitude to pour forth from us in a mighty way. Break our hearts where your heart is broken, and help us live a lifestyle of compassion, mercy, and generosity in Jesus' name. Amen.

Workaholic Ethic

34

> Therefore, while the promise of entering his rest is still open, let us take care that none of you should seem to have failed to reach it. For indeed the good news came to us just as to them; but the message they heard did not benefit them, because they were not united by faith with those who listened. For we who have believed enter that rest, just as God has said,
>
> "As in my anger I swore,
> 'They shall not enter my rest,' "
> though his works were finished at the foundation of the world.
>
> So then, a Sabbath rest still remains for the people of God; for those who enter God's rest also cease from their labors as God did from his.
>
> —Hebrews 4:1-3, 9-10
> (Read Hebrews 4:1-10)

Many seemingly positive cultural values eat away at youth workers, but few are as subtly devastating as the workaholic ethic. Most congregations reward busy-ness far more than they reward stillness. They seek crowds over solitude, honor high-energy over silence, and prefer activity to rest.

The truth of the matter is that some of this active, high-energy, crowd-pleasing work is necessary if we're going to keep getting a paycheck. After all, churches aren't paying our salaries so that we can go be alone with God all of the time. They want us ministering to kids.

There's a balance between busy-ness and sabbath that is sometimes very difficult to find. On one hand, we know that our relationship with God is pivotal in our being effective ministers. If we busy ourselves with programming and administrative tasks without tending the fires of our own souls, our effectiveness will diminish and we will set ourselves up for burnout.

On the other hand, tending to our spiritual needs is not only hard to measure and account for, but it's also not what most churches pay youth ministers to do. After all, we expect others to grow in their faith on top of their day-to-day obligations, whether a full-time job, family obligations, and civic responsibilities (including the church) for the adults, or school, extracurricular activities, family time, and youth ministry activities for young people.

We must differentiate our own spiritual health from our youth ministry job— whether we're volunteers or paid staff members. Our level of success or failure in retreat planning, fundraising, or small group leadership is just a measurement of how well we're performing those specific tasks. In and of themselves, these tasks do not define how well our youth ministries are ushering students into deeper

Will Penner

relationships with Christ. And how well we carry out these tasks certainly doesn't determine our own worth as disciples of Christ.

Theologically, we know that we can't earn our salvation—but that doesn't keep us from trying sometimes. We may not verbally preach a works-based doctrine to our youth, but our actions sometimes do.

Resting from our work isn't just about taking a vacation day, though giving ourselves a day off is good to do from time to time. Frankly, if we don't find some rest in our faith—specifically in the knowledge that God's love transcends what we do or don't do, and what our kids do and don't do—then something is wrong with our theology. We must not be anxious about earning God's favor. We can't earn it, no matter what; it's already been bestowed.

And if we're busy trying to be top-notch youth workers just to earn the favor of others, then, well, we need to knock it off. We need to be faithful to fulfill whatever job description we've agreed to (or work to change the description if it's unreasonable or be faithful to God's calling us elsewhere if it's unreasonable and unchangeable); doing so is good stewardship of the task we've been assigned. But we need to take sabbath just as seriously. A body cannot function long without physical rest. And neither can a spirit.

"Remember the sabbath . . . and keep it holy" (Exodus 20:8).

Challenge: Look for creative ways to keep the sabbath. Take a fifteen-minute nap every day. Make a ninety-minute lunch appointment with God each week in the park and leave your planner at the office. Turn off your television for a week, and don't replace it with anything. Learn an ancient, contemplative prayer practice and incorporate it into your regular rhythm. Say no to something.

Prayer: Lord, relieve the anxiety we feel about trying to earn the respect or admiration of others. These persons are not our masters; you are. May we find rest in knowing that you already love us more than we can possibly imagine and that you're taking care of the kids in our youth ministry too.

35 Serve Only Him: Claimed As God's Own

> Jesus, full of the Holy Spirit, returned from the Jordan and was led by the Spirit in the wilderness, where for forty days he was tempted by the devil.
>
> —Luke 4:1-2a
> (Read Luke 4:1-13)

Occasionally, we hear accounts of persons who have suffered amnesia. Sometimes they have lost their memory after an accident. But often, especially in the cases of persons with Alzheimer's disease, these persons have lost their very sense of identity. They literally do not know any longer who they are, and they depend on those who care for them to hold that identity for them. Amnesia also takes other, more subtle forms. United Methodist Bishop and former Professor at Duke Divinity School, Will Willimon, tells a story from his teen-age years about his mother's parting words to him one night on the driveway as he pulled out to head downtown for an evening with his friends: "Remember who you are, Will." Willimon laughs about the mild sting of that reminder and the challenge it put to him of holding onto his deepest sense of integrity as a disciple of Jesus amid the many temptations to "spiritual amnesia" in his social life as a young man.

All of us, young or older, face such temptations daily. Media experts estimate that the average American is subject to about three thousand marketing messages a day that aim to define them in a certain way. These messages scream at us: "You are what you drive," "...what you wear," "...what you eat," and so forth. They seek to claim us for the world, to define us strictly as consumers and producers. There are also deep-seated messages that we internalize from family, school, and work about our sense of worth being dependent on what we do. Something in us strongly believes that we are what we do, how well we do, and how much we do. Even in ministry, we face the temptation of spiritual amnesia—forgetting that we have already been redeemed and claimed as beloved daughters and sons whose worth depends only on God's love, not on anything we do.

Luke tells us that, after Jesus' baptism in the Jordan and full awakening to his messianic identity as God's beloved Son, Jesus was led by the Spirit into the wilderness where he was tempted by the devil. Satan is essentially attempting to inflict amnesia on Jesus—to divert him from his sense of identity as God's Son. The devil is devious in his method, seeking to place conditions on the unique status and mission given to Jesus. "If you are the beloved Son, turn these stones into loaves" (verse 3). Do something relevant so that you can prove to others and yourself that you have real power, real value in the "real" world. Satan seeks to claim Jesus for himself by promising him all the power of the world (verses 5-7).

Michael Hryniuk

Jesus says no. Satan challenges him to throw himself off the pinnacle of the temple, to do something spectacular (verses 9-11). Jesus refuses to put God to the test. At every turn, Jesus is challenged to remember who he is. In every case he returns to the awareness of the immense love he has experienced through his relation to the Father. This knowledge of God's love claims him. It is his shield and sword in the spiritual warfare he faces. His passionate desire to be one with the Father grounds him in his sense of whose he really is.

Those of us in youth ministry know well the struggle with temptations. Even though we have felt that burning desire for closeness to God, many other desires and fears seek to claim us and overwhelm us, causing us to forget our deepest name as beloved. Even when we have heard our name spoken as God's beloved son or daughter, we succumb to the false naming of the world. We continually slip into spiritual amnesia. Jesus reminds us here of the way through temptation and of the continual need to return with him to the Father—to be reclaimed by the presence and power of God's unconditional love and to hear God say "Do not fear, for I have redeemed you; I have called you by name, you are mine" (Isaiah 43:1b). No matter how often we forget our deepest name as beloved, the Spirit is sent to us to reclaim us. All we need to do is open ourselves again to the love that heals us and reminds us of who we truly are.

Prayer: Lord, you search us and know us. You know when we slip into spiritual amnesia and forget who we truly are. You know when we are distracted by the false naming of the world and tempted to prove ourselves and our worth by succumbing to the seductions of security, power, and success. Help us today to be open to the power of your unconditional grace, remind us of who are, and reclaim us for you alone. Through the power of the cross and Resurrection, lead us back with Christ to the truth of our lives, and empower us to reclaim others in Christ's holy name. Amen.

36 You Are My Son: Named As Beloved

> Now, when all the people were baptized, and when
> Jesus also had been baptized and was praying, the heaven
> was opened, and the Holy Spirit descended upon him in bodily
> form like a dove. And a voice came from heaven, "You are my Son,
> the Beloved; with you I am well pleased."
>
> —Luke 3:21-22

Have you ever pondered the power of your own name? The name we carry from birth are so much a part of us that we easily forget how much weight it carries. We are reminded at times how potent the sound of our name is when a loved one speaks it with tenderness or, perhaps, frustration! We feel the importance of our name when it is proclaimed on solemn occasions such as weddings or graduations; but our name always carries a certain sacred meaning. In the Bible, God's name is so holy that it cannot even be uttered. In many stories, persons receive new names at moments of sacred encounter or spiritual transition—Abram becomes Abraham, Simon becomes Peter, and Saul becomes Paul. In the early church, persons were healed through the invocation of the name of Jesus Christ.

In this passage from Luke, Jesus is praying after his baptism in the Jordan, when heaven opens, the Holy Spirit descends upon him, and a voice says, "You are my Son, the Beloved; with you I am well pleased" (verse 22b). At this moment, Jesus awakens in a definitive way to his messianic name: the Christ, the Anointed One of God. The power of the Holy Spirit descends upon him and he hears the Father's voice within him and around him revealing his deepest identity as the Beloved Son in whom the Father delights. This is the moment at which Jesus of Nazareth comes to know himself in a unique way as the Servant of God, the chosen one sent to bring forth justice to the nations. Jesus hears this name spoken in the depths of his soul and is empowered to go forth in his public ministry to others.

What does this moment mean for those of us who are ministers of Christ to young people? The great Anglican archbishop Desmond Tutu of Capetown, South Africa, was once addressing a group of senior theological students in a large American seminary. He congratulated them for their many years of study and their mastery of disciplines such as systematic theology, biblical studies, and church history. But, he told them that, as they prepared to minister to others in Christ's name, they had to understand that they actually knew nothing of any great value if they didn't know in their hearts that they were beloved of

Michael Hryniuk

the Father. If they knew this name as beloved in the depths of their being, as Christ did, then they would be able to minister in God's name by the power of the Holy Spirit. If they didn't know this, then all of their learned words would ring hollow and have no real power to change lives.

Bishop Tutu announced that, in the course that he was about to teach, he would simply tell the students one story after another about how God had revealed this name to him and how God had loved him into the fullness of life and ministry to others. For Bishop Tutu there was nothing sentimental about hearing his name spoken as beloved of God. It had empowered him to lead his people through one of the most difficult and violent periods of South African history, help liberate his country from the evil of apartheid, and foster forgiveness and healing in the aftermath. For Desmond Tutu, knowing his name as beloved was the foundation of his whole ministry.

We too are invited to listen deeply in prayer every day and to hear our name spoken as beloved of the Father. We too have been baptized into Christ and have received a new identity that flows from being adopted as God's beloved daughter or son in whom God takes delight. Let us commit ourselves today to receiving fully the power of this name and to living in the joy and peace that come from knowing who we most truly are. The greatest sin is to refuse this love that names us and frees us to cry out with our brother Jesus, "Abba, Father!" Let us rest in the awareness of this love that holds us and sustains us at the core of our being and allows us to embrace ourselves, even in all of our beauty and brokenness. Finally, let us minister to young people in a way that reveals to them who they are as God's beloved, trusting in the power of God's Spirit to free them for the fullness of life in Christ.

Prayer: Holy Father, send your Spirit upon us this day that we might hear our name spoken as beloved and deepen at every moment an awareness of your delight in us. Help us to know ourselves, with Christ, as your sons and daughters, and empower us to reveal to others your immense love for them. We ask you this in name of Christ, your beloved Son. Amen.

37 Sent to Proclaim Release

Then Jesus, filled with the power of the Spirit, returned to Galilee, and a report about him spread throughout the surrounding country. He began to teach in their synagogues and was praised by every one.

When he came to Nazareth, where he had been brought up, he went to the synagogue on the sabbath day, as was his custom. He stood up to read, and the scroll of the prophet Isaiah was given to him. He unrolled the scroll and found the place where it is written:

"The Spirit of the Lord is upon me,
> because he has anointed me to bring good news to the poor.
He has sent me to proclaim release to the captives
> and recovery of sight to the blind,
>> to let the oppressed go free,
to proclaim the year of the Lord's favor."

And he rolled up the scroll, gave it back to the attendant, and sat down. The eyes of all were fixed on him. Then he began to say to them, "Today this scripture has been fulfilled in your hearing."

—Luke 4:14-21

Just recently my wife was offered a great job, one for which she had been waiting and hoping a long time. The job offer was wonderful news for her and she couldn't wait to share the news with others. I was overjoyed too and also wanted to tell everyone I knew the news. Good news is like that: You want to spread it around as quickly as you can! Perhaps it is a marriage proposal, a new baby on the way, a promotion, or admission to a program or school that you've applied to. At such moments like, sharing the joy seems to be the most natural and spontaneous reaction.

In this gospel passage, we hear that Jesus, "filled with the power of the Spirit," returns to his own people in Galilee to teach and preach in their synagogues. After being named and claimed as God's Beloved, after being tried and tempted in the desert, Jesus moves naturally and spontaneously toward sharing this "good news" with others. We don't really say what this "good news" is. In announcing his messianic identity and mission to his people, he uses the words of the prophet Isaiah: "The Spirit of the Lord is upon me, because he has anointed me to bring good news to the poor. He has sent me to proclaim release to the captives and recovery of sight to the blind, to let the oppressed go free"

Michael Hryniuk

(Luke 4:18, quoting Isaiah 61:1). The Spirit of God is burning in him, sending him to proclaim this good news to his brothers and sisters, to anoint them with the knowledge that they are beloved, and to free them from the oppression and blindness that is their condition apart from that powerful awareness of God's love.

Having experienced being named and claimed as God's beloved in baptism, we too have been called and sent with the power of the Spirit to share this good news with others—especially our young people. The word *christ* means the anointed one and those of us baptized into Christ have been anointed with God's love and sent to anoint others in God's name, to reveal God's love to them, and to free them from the burden of alienation from themselves, others, and God.

Jean Vanier, the founder of L'Arche communities for the intellectually disabled, once defined "love" as the capacity each of us has to reveal the beauty of others to themselves. To reveal another's beauty and giftedness to her or him is to anoint that person in the deepest possible way and liberate her or him to live the life of grace, peace, and joy that is the birthright of all God's children. But as we know in ministry, we cannot give what we have not received. To be sent with Christ as ministers of his love means learning the art (as Christ himself did) of continually receiving God's anointing everyday in prayer, Scripture, and the fellowship of believers. It means learning to tune in to that inner voice of love that seeks to reveal how we are beautiful and beloved in God's eyes and that empowers us to tell others the good news. Knowing God's joy in us, is good news to share indeed.

Prayer: Father, Son, and Spirit, you send us as your messengers and ministers of love. You send us as your beloved to anoint others in the name of Christ, to reveal their beauty to them, and to free them to live in the joy and peace that comes from knowing who they really are. Help us this day to open ourselves to your love and to your call for us that we might receive the anointing of your Spirit and offer the Spirit's anointing to others. We ask you this in Jesus' name. Amen

38 In My Father's House: Living Our Deepest Desire

Now every year his parents went to Jerusalem for the festival of the Passover. And when he was twelve years old, they went up as usual for the festival. When the festival was ended and they started to return, the boy Jesus stayed behind in Jerusalem, but his parents did not know it. Assuming that he was in the group of travelers, they went a day's journey. Then they started to look for him among their relatives and friends. When they did not find him, they returned to Jerusalem to search for him. After three days they found him in the temple, sitting among the teachers, listening to them and asking them questions. And all who heard him were amazed at his understanding and his answers. When his parents saw him they were astonished; and his mother said to him, "Child, why have you treated us like this? Look, your father and I have been searching for you in great anxiety." He said to them, "Why were you searching for me? Did you not know that I must be in my Father's house? But they did not understand what he said to them.

—Luke 2:41-50

When we look deeply into our hearts as ministers, we begin to discover that we are creatures of desire. Obviously, we enter into ministry because we desire to serve God, others, and the church—especially the young people whom God has placed in our care. When we reflect on our call, we also might notice some of the desires that are harder to understand and even admit: the desires to please others, to continuously help them, to gain their approval and acceptance. Then there are the deepest desires of our hearts: the desires for survival and security, for pleasure, to make our "mark" and prove our worth to ourselves and others who matter to us. When we are honest, we must admit that our lives and ministries are motivated fundamentally by this "tangle" of sometimes conflicted and confused desires. How do we sort out which we should follow? As always, it is helpful to look at the life of Christ.

In the Scripture above Luke's gospel gives us our first glimpse of the deep desire that motivated and guided Jesus in his life and ministry. After celebrating the annual Passover festival in Jerusalem with his family, Jesus is moved by the Holy Spirit to linger for a few extra days in the Temple courts with the teachers and elders who welcome and receive him with amazement. When his justifiably anxious parents discover him after a three day search and ask him why he has put them through such a harrowing experience, Jesus

Michael Hryniuk

responds (as he often does) with a question of his own: "Why were you searching for me? Did you not know that I must be in my Father's house?" (2:49). What is revealed here for the first time is Jesus' awareness of himself not only as the son of Mary and Joseph, but as the Son of God whose deepest desire is to be in his Father's house. This is the desire that will remain at the source of all that Jesus says and does in his life, mission, and ministry.

What about us? Is this desire to be with God at the heart of our lives and ministries? Or is it lost amid the pressures and strains of our daily schedules or covered over by other supposedly more "urgent" desires that we think we need to fulfill? Today, we are invited again to make contact with that deepest desire that burns in our hearts to be in communion with the Father through Christ. The psalmist knew this deepest desire when he exclaimed, "As a deer longs for flowing streams, so my soul longs for you, O God" (Psalms 42:1). To be in touch with the desire to be in God's presence is to be in touch with the deepest cry of our being—a being created in the image and likeness of God, who desires our love more than anything else in creation. Jesus expresses this desire best when he exhorts his disciples to "Strive first for the kingdom of God and his righteousness and all these things will be given to you as well" (Matthew 6:33). Only when we are in touch with this deepest desire for the Father are we empowered to awaken it in others. Jesus knew this and invites us to experience his desire for the Father so that we too might lead others— especially our young people—toward a relationship with Christ.

Prayer: Heavenly Father, we ask you to inflame the desire of our hearts for you and you alone. Through the power of your Spirit, help us become more like your son Jesus, whose passion and desire for you was at the heart of his life and mission. Help us to be witnesses to that desire in all that we say and do today so that others might come to know you, love you, and desire to live in your house forever. Amen

39 Commanding the Unclean Spirits

> He went down to Capernaum, a city in Galilee, and was teaching them on the sabbath. They were astounded at his teaching, because he spoke with authority. In the synagogue, there was a man who had the spirit of an unclean demon, and he cried out with a loud voice, "Let us alone! What have you to do with us, Jesus of Nazareth? Have you come to destroy us? I know who you are, the Holy One of God." But Jesus rebuked him, saying "Be silent, and come out of him!" When the demon had thrown him down before them, he came out of him without having done him any harm. They were all amazed and kept saying to one another, "What kind of utterance is this? For with authority and power he commands the unclean spirits, and out they come! And a report about him began to reach every place in the region.

> —Luke 4:31-37

Most of us in youth ministry would not likely remember the last time we cast out a demon. In our present day culture and congregations we tend to relegate demons and demon possession to the realm of horror movies and ghost stories. Certainly, we might acknowledge rare cases in which a teen or adult gets caught in the nightmare of satanic worship and its consequences, and we might even wonder about some of our own flock sometimes, especially when they start wearing black, piercing their bodies, and listening to bands that promote rage, hatred, and violence. But, we might think, real demonic possession only happens in extreme cases and it seldom occurs in our communities. When it does, there are medical and psychological experts who know how to deal with it. Casting out demons is almost certainly not part of our job description.

In this passage from Luke's Gospel Jesus is involved in an electrifying encounter with a man suffering demonic possession. After announcing his messianic mission of proclaiming the good news in his hometown of Nazareth and meeting the hostility of the people there, Jesus is immediately confronted in the neighboring town of Capernaum by a person who is crying out for release from captivity and oppression by an evil, or unclean, spirit. The Anointed One is called upon, not only to announce the good news, but also to heal and anoint others in their brokenness. He rebukes the evil spirit and calls it out with an authority and power that the people of Capernaum have never seen before. This sabbath healing and exorcism reveals Christ's power to command forces that his contemporaries feared most: the demonic forces of darkness and destruction against which they felt powerless.

Michael Hryniuk

As followers of Christ, are we not also called and sent to be healers? Are we not also called to confront what binds and oppresses others and anoint them in their places of brokenness? In our tendency to relegate demonic possession to the realm of the supernatural, we are prone to forget that many instances of more ordinary, garden-variety possession can take over our lives and the lives we care for. There is some broken part of each of us that resists and refuses God's love. This part of us needs to be healed.

Busy-ness, stress, anger, and despair are some of the "unclean spirits" that creep into our lives and the lives of our young people. These spirits can oppress and bind us, slowly burning us out without our even being aware. They can make us deaf to the voice of the Father in us—the voice that is seeking to name us and claim us as beloved. Many spirits roaming around in our media-saturated culture also seek to falsely name and claim us, to distort our sense of identity and self-worth, and to drive us to distraction and sterility. These "spirits" may not have forked tails and pitchforks, but they are no less demonic. To cast out these demons, we need to recognize their presence and power and confront them as Jesus did: with the power and authority of Christ's love. Even more importantly, we need to open up the places in us that need to be healed and unbound by the Spirit of Christ. As one of the great Russian saints, Seraphim of Sarov, once said: "If you alone find inner peace, thousands around will be saved." Inner peace and joy are the fruits of this healing and empower us to be healers of others in the name of Jesus.

Prayer: Father, Son, and Spirit, by the power of your love you command the demons in our lives to come out. You free us from the bondage of sin, brokenness, and despair. Open us and heal us that we too might be agents of your healing love. Give us eyes and ears to discern where the "evil spirits" live in our world and especially in the world of our young people so that we can free them and claim them for you and your kingdom. We pray this in Jesus' name, Amen.

40 Crying

> As he came near and saw the city, he wept over it,
> saying, "If you, even you, had only recognized on
> this day the things that make for peace! But now
> they are hidden from your eyes.
> Then he entered the temple and began to drive out those who
> were selling things there; and he said, "It is written,
> 'My house shall be a house of prayer';
> but you have made it a den of robbers."
>
> —Luke 19:41-42, 45-46

You are on the frontlines of ministry.

You see the pain of the world that most people never encounter.

And it hurts.

You still feel that "service project high" after returning from a week of intimacy and mission with your youth, but you can't help but cry when you think about the pain that the youth shared:

- Abuse
- Cutting/self-mutilation
- Suicidal attempts
- Drugs
- Rape
- Eating disorders
- Suicidal thoughts
- Neglect by parents
- Sexual addictions
- Rejection and fear felt by the youth who thinks he might be gay

If you've been in youth ministry long enough, you realize just how much bad stuff is in this world; just how much pain people are willing to selfishly inflict on one another; just how hard it is to make sense of this world.

Our adolescents ask the question, but so do we—we scream it: "How can God let these things happen?"

Jesus entered Jerusalem with all the fanfare of a youth group returning from a week of service. People celebrated his return, were excited about what he had done since his last trip to Jerusalem, and could not wait to see what he might do next. Yet after this joyous celebration, Jesus weeps. He's seen the pain and the darkness of people's lives. He sees how the people of Jerusalem will continue to hurt others—even him. And he weeps.

Tears traced the outline of the Savior as they do us when we think about the horrible things that many of our youth have suffered. Like Jesus, we want to

Mike Baughman

run into the church and turn over the tables, take our anger out on that abusive father, yell at the senior pastor until she or he does something to fix the congregation that does not "get" what we do. We want to ride in on our white horse and fix whatever it is that is hurting the youth we love—the youth God loves—as if our actions would somehow make everything right.

Sometimes we can turn over the tables and sometimes we can't, but we are frequently left with questions and doubts inspired by the stuff of the world.

I will not offer any stale theory or complex theology to explain the world of hurt that presses down upon the adolescents of our world. But I do intend to offer hope.

I want you to know that other youth pastors also see just how bad the world can be and that we weep together. More importantly, Jesus saw and experienced just how bad the world can be and continues to weep with us. In moments of doubt, we wrestle alongside Christ who calls from the cross, "My God, my God, why have you forsaken me" (see Mark 15:34b, quoting Psalm 22:1).

Challenge: Find a fellow youth worker whom you can trust and share your struggles with. If you already have someone like this, write him or her a letter of thanks for being willing to cry with you.

Prayer: Precious Lord with tear-stained skin, weep with us and with our youth. Help us find comfort in your company and presence. Wash us with the tears of your love. Grant us the hope to continue, the fortitude to turn over the tables of hurt, and the place to weep when the job gets too hard. Thank you for your presence with us. Amen.

Youth Ministry
As Social Justice

47

>"Blessed are the poor in spirit, for theirs is the kingdom of heaven.
>
>"Blessed are those who mourn, for they will be comforted.
>
>"Blessed are the meek, for they will inherit the earth.
>
>"Blessed are those who hunger and thirst for righteousness, for they will be filled.
>
>"Blessed are the merciful, for they will receive mercy.
>
>"Blessed are the pure in heart, for they will see God.
>
>"Blessed are the peacemakers, for they will be called children of God.
>
>"Blessed are those who are persecuted for righteousness' sake, for theirs is the kingdom of heaven.
>
>"Blessed are you when people revile you and persecute you and utter all kinds of evil against you falsely on my account. Rejoice and be glad, for your reward is great in heaven, for in the same way they persecuted the prophets who were before you."
>
>—Matthew 5:1-12

Throughout college I was active in the Wesley Fellowship, a United Methodist campus ministry, at Duke University. At one of the richest schools in the world, our ministry had a very strong focus on social justice. Spring break was spent on the streets of Washington DC, the rooftops of Appalachian houses, and the hills of Honduras. Our time with the poor and oppressed had such a powerful impact on us that most of those in my graduating class who were active in the Wesley Fellowship went into some sort of ministry with the poor and oppressed. Brad went to Haiti to work with the Peace Corps, and Vicki took a job with Heifer Project International. Veronica went to Peru to work with an orphanage, and Tyler decided to live in a L'Arche community to learn from mentally disabled persons living in Christian communion.

I began work as the youth pastor in a suburban church in one of the ten wealthiest counties in the United States of America.

Sure, I was in ministry, but while my colleagues were running across the globe to care for the world's poor, oppressed, and disadvantaged, I left the Wesley Fellowship to minister to youth among the wealthiest one percent of the world's population. Could I really have been following the voice of the shepherd who called me to minister to the poor and oppressed?

Yes. Absolutely. We spend too much time thinking of social justice or mission work as a part of youth ministry and not nearly enough time thinking of youth ministry as social justice in its own right.

Mike Baughman

Youth ministry in affluent communities is one of the greatest fields for social justice ministry because it seeks to transform those who are most likely to become the oppressors in our society—the wealthiest of the wealthy—before they become so enmeshed in the systems of oppression that they hardly recognize how their actions affect the less fortunate. Mission work should be about more than just spiritual highs and feeling good about how much youth can do when they work hard for a week. Service offers so much more. Youth take their first steps toward breaking down patterns of oppression when they see how little they can do in one week and become more aware of how their lifestyle contributes to the poverty they encounter.

Youth ministry is social justice ministry because adolescents, regardless of how much money their families have, are among the poor and oppressed in the United States of America. Unsure of their own identity and wrestling with God, they are often the poor in spirit. Divorce, suicide, abuse, job instability for parents, and the loss of passionate relationships rank adolescents among those who mourn. Adolescents are among "the least of these" in our society, and the church has a responsibility to minister to them and care for them amid their chaotic lives.

- How are you challenging your youth to claim their role as world-changing peacemakers?
- In what ways do you discourage youth from acknowledging their own privilege through your actions, the church budget, or the focus of your ministry?
- In what ways are you encouraging youth to acknowledge their own privilege?

Challenge: Do you want your youth to inherit the kingdom of heaven? You are on the frontlines of social justice ministry. You get to participate in God's sanctifying work—work that transforms youth into those who "hunger for righteousness" and who may inspire the church by their willingness to be "persecuted for righteousness' sake."

Prayer: Lord Jesus Christ, we know that you will be walking into youth group this week for you are among the hungry, hurting, and lost. Grant us the vision to see you in the face of our youth. Grant us the ability to care for you in the form of hurting adolescents. Grant us the courage to challenge them to thirst for righteousness. And grant us the courage to accept that challenge ourselves. Amen.

42 Through the Valley

The LORD is my shepherd, I shall not want.
    He makes me lie down in green pastures;
he leads me beside still waters;
    he restores my soul.
He leads me in right paths
    for his name's sake.

Even though I walk through the darkest valley,
    I fear no evil;
for you are with me;
    your rod and your staff—
    they comfort me.

You prepare a table before me
    in the presence of my enemies;
you anoint my head with oil;
    my cup overflows.
Surely goodness and mercy shall follow me
    all the days of my life,
and I shall dwell in the house of the LORD
    my whole life long.

—Psalm 23

It was 3:30 in the morning when she woke up. She was with her youth on a service project. Doing the standard bed-scan that all youth pastors do if they wake up at such a late hour, she noticed that a few of the youth were missing from their beds. Annoyed and angry that they would be out of their sleeping bags at this hour, she plodded her way down the hallway to the common area. Just before barging into the room, however, she stopped. She heard the voices of her five missing youth—praying. They were praying for her.

Two nights prior she had revealed to them that she had separated from her husband because he was abusive. For the past two nights, these youth had stayed up and met to pray for her without her even knowing. She was in the "valley of the shadow of death" and her youth were helping to pray her through it.

Psalm 23 talks about the "valley of the shadow of death" (see verse 4, KJV), but what is this valley? A valley is a low place of uncertainty from which we cannot see the future and in which we are caught up in the stress of our lives. Shadows obscure where we are headed. "Death" may refer to the death of our old lifestyle or the death of something that made us happy or the death of our bodies or the death of a loved one. In this valley we hear words such as:

Mike Baughman

- Despair
- Fear
- Change
- Sadness
- Pain

I'm sure that these and other words of the valley have, at one time, echoed in the chambers of your heart. They very well may be rattling around in your soul right now. Maybe you see the valley coming up ahead. So how do we make it through the valley of the shadow of death? We need prayer to help us follow the voice of the shepherd who does not leave us.

The youth in the story above helped pray their youth pastor through the valley! We certainly need to pray for ourselves when we find ourselves confronted by the shadows, but we also need others to pray us through when our legs are weary and souls are tired. Who are you going to ask to pray you through the valleys of your life? I'm sure you are wonderful at praying for others who are passing through their lives' darkest valleys, but in whom are you willing to confide those words that echo from the valley of your heart?

Challenge: List the people whom you would trust to pray you through the dark valleys of your life. Then circle those whom you can tell the details of your struggles. Spend some time in prayer, looking over the list, and thanking God for each of these persons. If you feel that you do not have enough names on your list, have conversations with others whom you feel you can trust.

Prayer: Shepherd God, we humbly ask you to guide us through the valleys of our lives. Send us angels to pray us through as we listen for the sound of your voice and find comfort in your rod and staff. Thank you for the comfort and confidence of the psalmist's words that we walk "through" the valley and not "into" it. Thank you for the privilege to walk with others through the valleys of their lives. Guide our feet and know our hearts. Amen.

43 Go Ahead, Make an Ass, er . . . a Donkey out of Yourself!

God's anger was kindled because (Balaam) was going, and the angel of the LORD took his stand in the road as his adversary. Now he was riding on the donkey, and his two servants were with him. The donkey saw the angel of the LORD standing in the road, with a drawn sword in his hand; so the donkey turned off the road, and went into the field; and Balaam struck the donkey, to turn it back onto the road. Then the angel of the LORD stood in a narrow path between the vineyards, with a wall on either side. When the donkey saw the angel of the LORD, it scraped against the wall, and scraped Balaam's foot against the wall; so he struck it again. Then the angel of the LORD went ahead, and stood in a narrow place, where there was no way to run either to the right or to the left. When the donkey saw the angel of the LORD, it lay down under Balaam; and Balaam's anger was kindled, and he struck the donkey with his staff. Then the LORD opened the mouth of the donkey, and it said to Balaam, "What have I done to you, that you have struck me these three times?" Balaam said to the donkey, "Because you have made a fool of me! I wish I had a sword in my hand! I would kill you right now!" But the donkey said to Balaam, "Am I not your donkey, which you have ridden all your life to this day? Have I been in the habit of treating you this way?" And he said, "No."

Then the LORD opened the eyes of Balaam, and he saw the angel of the LORD standing in the road, with his drawn sword in his hand; and he bowed down, falling on his face.

—Numbers 22:22–31
(*Read Numbers 22*)

He stood at our door with a perplexed look on his face. From the expression on his face and the tears in his eyes, I could tell that something wasn't quite right. "Hey," he said, "My car is up the street and it got pretty messed up. I need to come in and calm down for a minute and then call someone for help." After a few minutes we walked down the street to see his car. In a fit of anger he had chased after some other kids and rammed his car into a high curb. The damage to the car was pretty severe but, thankfully, no one had been hurt.

While we waited for AAA to come tow his car and for his mom to come pick him up, we had a long talk about warning signs, second chances, and God's

Drew Dyson

invitation to come home. The truth is that we'd had similar conversations several times before this incident. I knew that he was on a path that would lead to more hurt and pain, but I was having a hard time convincing him of that. All I could do was continue to be there and remind him that I loved him, that God loved him, and that he could always "return home."

Balak, king of the Moabites, had summoned Balaam, a soothsayer from Pethor, to call down a curse on the people of Israel to drive them back from Canaan. Hearing the word of God, Balaam initially refused to make the journey back to the king. However, after more convincing from Balak's emissaries, Balaam set out for Moab to deliver the curse for the king. He saddled his donkey and headed out.

Once Balaam hit the road God's anger was kindled, and God sent an angel to block Balaam's path. Three times the donkey saw the angel and tried to keep Balaam from moving forward. All three times Balaam beat the donkey and pushed it into continuing the trek. Danger was to be found where Balaam was headed and the donkey knew it.

How many times have you had to stand in the unenviable position of the path between a young person headed in the wrong direction and the certain destruction ahead? Committing yourself to being a mentor, a teacher, and a guide for young people will certainly lead to more than one occasion when you will be called on by God to "make an ass out of yourself." And almost as certainly, pain will be involved.

It is not easy to stand in the world of young people and shine the light of Christ on the dark and dangerous places. It is not easy when a young person makes unwise choices that you know will lead them down treacherous paths. It is not easy to stand in the way, because you end up feeling beaten up and trampled down.

Take heart! Do not be afraid! You don't stand in those treacherous places alone. God is with you and will provide you with the courage to stand firm, the words to comfort, and the glue to put back together the broken pieces. Your persistence, your patience, and your prayers will make a world of difference in the life of each young person that you stand with. Go ahead— make an ass out of yourself!

Prayer Focus: Young people who are facing difficult and dangerous choices.

44 When the Nets Are Empty

After these things Jesus showed himself again to the disciples by the Sea of Tiberius; and he showed himself in this way. Gathered there together were Simon Peter, Thomas called the Twin, Nathanael of Cana in Galilee, the sons of Zebedee, and two others of his disciples. Simon Peter said to them, "I am going fishing." They said to him, "We will go with you." They went out and got into the boat, but that night they caught nothing.

Just after daybreak, Jesus stood on the beach; but the disciples did not know that it was Jesus. Jesus said to them, "Children, you have no fish, have you?" They answered him, "No." He said to them, "Cast the net to the right side of the boast, and you will find some." So they cast it and now they were not able to haul it in because there were so many fish. That disciple whom Jesus loved said to Peter, "It is the Lord!" When Simon Peter heard that it was the Lord, he put on some clothes, for he was naked, and jumped into the sea. But the other disciples came in the boat, dragging the net full of fish, for they were not far from the land, only about a hundred yards off.

—John 21:1-8
(*Read John 21:1-14*)

It really is embarrassing to be known as the one who never catches anything. For several years we would take our youth to the shore home of a member of our congregation who owned a large fishing boat. Each year we would go out in groups of eight to fish in the great Atlantic. And each year I wouldn't catch a thing—not a fish, not a shoe, not a cold—nothing! The last straw came when I was on the boat with seven sixth-graders who were pulling in bluefish like *Sesame Street's* Bert and Ernie, yelling, "Here fishy, fishy, fishy," while all the while I—with a sonar fish finder, the best pole that money could buy, and my grandfather's lucky hat—came up empty.

You've been there too. Can't you hear yourself echoing Peter: "Master, I've worked all night long but the nets are still empty"; "Master, I've done everything I can but I'm still wiped out"; "Master, I'm at the end of my rope and I don't know if I can hold on any longer." The truth is, we all know what empty nets feel like.

Emptiness comes from all sorts of places. Some of us have grown tired and fatigued and are at the end of our ropes. In such instances burnout is no longer a thing to be avoided but a thing to be rescued from. We're empty.

Drew Dyson

Some of us have had to deal with failure one too many times. Maybe the church board doesn't like the way things are going with the youth ministry; the parents don't like the cost of the mission trips; and no matter how hard we try, the youth won't show up for anything but lock-ins and outings. We're empty. Then there's the disappointment of the new job that wasn't all that it was cracked up to be, the relationship that isn't working, or the friendship that has been broken over a petty argument. We all know what it means to have an empty net.

The good news is that it is often during the most intense periods of fruitlessness that Jesus Christ reveals his power and during the times of darkness that God sheds the greatest light. It was when Lazarus lay dead in a tomb that Jesus Christ was revealed as the one who had power over death (John 11:1-44). It was when two heart-broken men walked away from Jerusalem on the road to Emmaus that Jesus was revealed in the breaking of the bread (Luke 24:13-35). And it was when Peter was fishing on a familiar beach that the risen Jesus was revealed when the nets that had been empty all night long came up bursting with fish.

I don't know if your nets are empty right now or why. You may be burned out by busy-ness and doing the right thing but leaving little time for being the person you have been created to be. You may be holding on to failures of your past—real or perceived—such as not being a good enough parent, not caring enough for your own parents, not meeting the expectations of your spouse. Or you may be carrying the burden of not being able to forgive—either yourself or someone who has hurt you. In our periods of intense darkness, the clear call comes: "Cast your net to the other side and God will show up!"

Affirmation: Hear the good news: Cast your nets to the other side of the boat and receive the grace of God that is waiting for you. Fear not, for you are not alone.

45 A Simple Table

When the hour came, he took his place at the table, and the apostles with him. He said to them, "I have eagerly desired to eat this Passover with you before I suffer; for I tell you, I will not eat it until it is fulfilled in the kingdom of God." Then he took a cup, and after giving thanks he said, "Take this and divide it among yourselves; for I tell you that from now on I will not drink of the fruit of the vine until the kingdom of God comes." Then he took a loaf of bread, and when he had given thanks, he broke it and gave it to them, saying, "This is my body, which is given for you. Do this in remembrance of me." And he did the same with the cup after supper, saying, "This cup that is poured out for you is the new covenant in my blood."

—Luke 22:14-20
(*Read Luke 22:14-23*)

It's a rather simple table. Made of plain two-by-fours, glued and nailed together by my father and uncle, and covered by years' worth of polyurethane coats, the table has been in the family for more than thirty years. The simple table holds so many memories for me, my brothers, my cousins, and now another generation of children.

There was the time when my brothers and cousin wrapped up a dead snake and gave it to my aunt for her birthday. There was the time when another of my cousins reached across a burning candle and dropped the hot-off-the-stove gravy onto my lap. There was the time when the family gathered around the table for the first dinner after my sister died. This simple table has seen its share of laughter, tears, angry words, and hugs. But one thing is sure—around that table we were claimed, commissioned, and connected.

We were claimed because we knew that we were Dysons and Fischers. And anyone who gathered around that table with us was not a stranger or a guest, but for that time they were part of our family.

We were commissioned because it was around that table that we learned to behave like Dysons. We knew what was expected of us and we were held accountable for our actions.

We were connected because, no matter where we spent our day, we were always home for dinner. As the years went by and we were separated by miles, years, and lifestyles, when we gathered around that table, we were home and were always welcomed as part of the family.

Drew Dyson

Two thousand years ago, the disciples gathered around a similarly simple table and shared a simple meal. Each week or month, modern disciples gather around a similar table for an even simpler meal of bread and wine. And at that table we are also claimed, commissioned, and connected.

By laying down his life and pouring out his blood for us, Jesus has claimed us as God's children. The prophet Isaiah makes clear that the people of Israel have been claimed by God: "This is what the Lord says—he who created you, O Jacob, he who formed you, O Israel: 'Fear not, for I have redeemed you; I have called you by name; you are mine' " (Isaiah 43:1, NIV).

Around God's table we are also commissioned. The liturgy of my tradition, in the prayer of consecration of the elements, says: "Pour out your Holy Spirit on us gathered here and on these gifts of bread and wine. Make them be for us the body and blood of Christ that we may be for the world the body of Christ, redeemed by his blood" (from *The United Methodist Hymnal*, page 14). When we receive the elements and accept the grace of Jesus Christ, we also accept the responsibility for living the life of faith: seeking justice, doing mercy, and walking humbly with our God (see Micah 6:8). Like our spiritual ancestor, Abraham, we are blessed to be a blessing (see Genesis 12:1-3).

Finally, at the table we are connected as the body of Christ. When I was leaving a church after serving seven years as youth minister, we closed with a very memorable Holy Communion service. It was that holy meal that helped all of us to remember that no matter where we went, no matter how far we traveled, we would always be joined together because of the gift of Jesus Christ through the elements of Communion.

Youth Ministry, as Kenda Dean makes clear in her book *Practicing Passion* (Eerdmans, 2004), must center itself around the passion of Jesus Christ in order to connect with the passion of adolescents struggling to make their way in a shattered world. When we celebrate the Eucharist with our youth, we help them to take hold of their identities as Christ's own, whom Christ has claimed, commissioned, and connected.

Challenge: Find a way to incorporate the celebration of Holy Communion into your ministry with young people. Perhaps you can have small groups of youth over for dinner at your house and invite your pastor to share the Eucharist with you. Perhaps you can make a simple Communion table the centerpiece of your youth room.

46 · A Willing Sacrifice?

After these things God tested Abraham. He said to him, "Abraham!" And he said, "Here I am." He said, "Take your son, your only son Isaac, whom you love, and go to the land of Moriah, and offer him there as a burnt offering on one of the mountains that I shall show you." So Abraham rose early in the morning, saddled his donkey, and took two of his young men with him, and his son Isaac; he cut the wood for the burnt offering, and set out and went to the place in the distance that God had shown him. . . . Isaac said to his father Abraham, "Father!" And he said, "Here I am, my son." He said, "The fire and the wood are here, but where is the lamb for a burnt offering?" Abraham said, "God himself will provide the lamb for a burnt offering, my son." So the two of them walked on together.

When they came to the place that God had shown him, Abraham built an altar there and laid the wood in order. He bound his son Isaac, and laid him on the altar, on top of the wood. Then Abraham reached out his hand and took the knife to kill his son. But the angel of the LORD called to him from heaven, and said, "Abraham, Abraham!" And he said, "Here I am." He said, "Do not lay your hand on the boy or do anything to him; for now I know that you fear God, since you have not withheld your son, your only son, from me." And Abraham looked up and saw a ram, caught in a thicket by its horns. Abraham went and took the ram and offered it up as a burnt offering instead of his son. So Abraham called that place "The LORD will provide"; as it is said to this day, "On the mount of the LORD it shall be provided."

—Genesis 22:1-3, 7-14

I watched it happen too many times to too many friends. It happened in my own family when I was growing up. I've been close before, but thankfully God has always provided me with a resounding alarm to wake me from my foolish pursuits.

For Abraham, the command from God was clear: "Take your son, your only son Isaac, whom you love, and go to the land of Moriah, and offer him there as a burnt offering on one of the mountains that I shall show you" (verse 2). Abraham's faithfulness and holy desire to please God led him to lay his beloved son on a makeshift altar and raise the knife that could both honor God and rip out Abraham's heart.

Drew Dyson

For most of us in youth ministry, the call of God is equally clear. We are called to open our lives to young people to share the good news of Jesus Christ. We are called to open our doors to the hurting youth whose home life is wrecked by violence. We are called to open our hearts to serve God by investing our time and talents in the lives of youth and families in our churches.

And on a makeshift altar lay our own families—our children, our spouses, our closest friends. Our quest for faithfulness, our holy desire to please God, and our pursuit for ministry excellence lead us to the altar. Every step of the way we pray that God will make another way. Unfortunately, for too many, the ram in the thicket comes too late. Our children, despite our efforts to pass on the faith, walk away from the church that they blame for taking their mother or father away. Our spouses simply have enough with competing with another lover—the ministry of the church—and give up hope.

The good news is that God has already provided a sacrifice in his son, Jesus Christ. The life, death, and resurrection of Jesus Christ makes clear that it is not our sacrifice that will save the lives of the young people we work with—it is his. We need to be able to walk away from the anxiety, guilt, and frustration of trying to save every young person; and we need to realize that God's grace is enough for them and for us.

Prayer Focus: God of grace and mercy, free me from my own ego and my inability to see the sacrifice that you have provided. Help me to not place the people who are closest to me on the altar of sacrifice. Help me to be a strong and loving parent, a faithful and attentive partner, and a loyal friend. Amen.

47 A Spoonful of Sugar

He called the crowd with his disciples, and said to them, "If any want to become my followers, let them deny themselves and take up their cross and follow me. For those who want to save their life will lose it, and those who lose their life for my sake, and for the sake of the gospel, will save it. For what will it profit them to gain the whole world and forfeit their life? Those who are ashamed of me and of my words in this adulterous and sinful generation, of them the Son of Man will also be ashamed when he comes in the glory of his Father with the holy angels.

—Mark 8:34-38
(Read Mark 8:27-38)

My daughter Allison hates to take medicine. Like most children, she detests the "medicine-y" taste of grape or cherry elixir. However, Allison takes her dislike of medicines to the extreme. Helping Allison take medicine is akin to getting a cat to take a bath, complete with fighting, hissing, and scratching.

One particularly miserable week, when the entire household was struggling with the flu, I had an epiphany. Standing wearily at the pharmacy counter I saw a sign that read, "Tired of the fight? Kids won't take their medicine? We have fifty-one flavors to help the medicine go down." Thank heavens for the little known merger between Johnson & Johnson and Baskin Robbins®! Who knew that a little chocolate or pineapple flavoring could bring a child running back for more!

That's how I feel about the above Scripture. This passage could use a flavored elixir—bubble gum, pineapple, something ... anything! Not because these words are difficult to understand—these are among the plainest, most direct of Jesus' words—but because they are the most difficult to swallow and to follow:

> "If any want to become my followers, let them deny themselves
> and take up their cross and follow me" (verse 34).

All of this talk of self-denial and sacrifice has no place in our culture. I mean, we are sensible people, and sensible people do not make such extraordinary demands on their lives. In our culture, church is often confused with some other social club—providing safe, wholesome activities for our children and a good base of friends to fill our needs for camaraderie and friendly interaction with others.

Church growth experts claim that the quickest way to increase a congregation's size is to remove any talk or notion of sacrifice and focus instead on what God

Drew Dyson

can do or provide for each individual person—prosperity, wholeness, self-esteem, and so on.

I like that. I can swallow that. Tastes a little bit like bubble gum. But a savior who just makes our lives easier and more comfortable doesn't bear any resemblance to Jesus, who demands our minds, our hearts, and our souls—who demands our all.

This Scripture is so hard because it calls us to bear the cross of Jesus; and we know what that means: sacrificial love, suffering, and even death. No thanks! I'll just take the McJesus Happy Meal®: Mediocre McNuggets®, feel-good fries, and a self-righteous shake.

Jesus calls us to deny ourselves, pick up our crosses, and follow him. Cross bearing has actually become a common part of our language. If someone we love has an illness and we are forced into the role of caregiver, if we have a difficult co-worker to deal with, or if one of our children is going through a rough patch we say, "Well, we all have our crosses to bear."

But the cross bearing Jesus calls us to has little to do with a situation in which we are forced to shoulder a difficult burden. Instead, Jesus is asking us to willingly and voluntarily take up our crosses and follow him.

The call of Jesus is a call to sacrificial love, to being a crossbearer. The crossbearer's motto is found in the words of Paul in 1 Corinthians. They may sound familiar:

"Crossbearers are patient, crossbearers are kind. They do not envy, they do not boast, they are not proud. Crossbearers are not rude, they are not self-seeking, they are not easily angered, they keep no record of wrongs. Crossbearers do not delight in evil but rejoice with the truth. They always protect, always trust, always hope, always persevere.
"The cross never fails."

—adapted from 1 Corinthians 13:4-8a, NIV

Prayer: Lord, help me to do away with short-selling and smooth-talking the demands of the gospel of Jesus Christ. Help me to pick up your cross and to accept the sacrificial call to love and to serve. Help me to willingly follow you.

48 The One Thing

"I tell you, there will be more joy in heaven over one sinner who repents than over ninety-nine righteous persons who need no repentance.

"Or what woman having ten silver coins, if she loses one of them, does not light a lamp, sweep the house, and search carefully until she finds it? When she has found it, she calls together her friends and neighbors, saying, 'Rejoice with me, for I have found the coin that I had lost.' Just so, I tell you, there is joy in the presence of the angels of God over one sinner who repents."

—Luke 15:7-10

A colleague and friend was recently telling me the story of a young woman from his congregation who had illuminated this familiar story in a fresh way. For years this young woman had interpreted this parable as many other faithful disciples have: She was the lost coin and Jesus, like the woman in the story, was willing to put everything aside to find her.

Digging deeper, however, she discovered that she was more like the woman in the story than the coin. Throughout her twenty-one rough years, she was aware that something was missing from her life, but she couldn't identify it, and she certainly couldn't find it. A deep sense of incompleteness nagged at her every time she risked serious personal reflection.

Night after night, month after month, year after year, she would sit at her kitchen table counting her coins. Three, four, five, six, seven, eight, nine . . . . That was it. Every day. This sense of emptiness was constantly a part of her life until the day she stepped into my friend's church. In that congregation she met other people who were searching for the same thing she was. And in the presence of those people, the body of Christ, God's light shined in Jesus Christ, and the young woman ran to the cross where she found her lost coin. The church was the place where she found God, the one thing—the only thing—that was missing from her life.

This young woman's insight into the parable of the lost coin may not bear the strict test of exegetical analysis, but it enabled her to stumble upon the meaning of the church. The church exists, not as a social club or a good-will agency, but as a place where all people can be supported in their search for the presence of God in their lives. The church is a place where lost people—sinners and tax collectors—can come and, in the presence of the light of Jesus Christ, find the one thing that's been missing from their lives.

Drew Dyson

Like this young woman, many of the young people in our churches and communities, are desperately searching for something that will make a difference in their lives, something that will give them meaning and purpose. Undoubtedly, they will not always be able to identify in a way such as that of my friend's parishioner, but the quest is the same.

The questions we must ask ourselves are clear:

- Are we providing a safe space where seekers and co-travelers can discover the very real presence of God in their lives?

- Is the God we point youth to worthy of their full fidelity?

- Do we believe and do we teach that commitment to Jesus Christ is more than a commitment to social responsibility or "niceness"?

- Can we help youth find "the one thing" that is missing from their lives? Or, more pointedly, can we put them in the way of grace so that Jesus Christ, "the one thing," can find them?

Prayer: God of grace and mercy, help us to be faithful in our ministry with young people. Help us to provide safe spaces where young people can search, question, and explore deep enough to find "the one thing" missing from their lives. Particularly, help _____ on (his or her) search. Make yourself known to all the youth in my ministry and help me to put them in the way of grace so that they might encounter you. Amen.

49 Daring to Be a Fool

The Message that points to Christ on the Cross
seems like sheer silliness to those hellbent on
destruction, but for those on the way of salvation
it makes perfect sense. This is the way God works, and
most powerfully as it turns out. It's written,
I'll turn conventional wisdom on its head,
I'll expose so-called experts as crackpots.
So where can you find someone truly wise, truly educated,
truly intelligent in this day and age? Hasn't God exposed it
all as pretentious nonsense? Since the world in all its fancy
wisdom never had a clue when it came to knowing God, God in
his wisdom took delight in using what the world considered
dumb—*preaching*, of all things!—to bring those who trust him
into the way of salvation.

—1 Corinthians 1:18-21 (*The Message*)

Do you remember when . . .

- dinosaurs came to life in your room?
- a magic wand could take away the pain of a cut or bruise?
- you became the heroes that you watched on television—G.I. Joe, Teenage Mutant Ninja Turtles, or basketball superstars?

Do you remember when . . .

- science turned dinosaurs into a thing of the past to be studied, not played with?
- the dreams that could be realized with the touch of a magic wand became silly childhood fantasies?
- athletes became overpaid, obnoxious millionaires?

Somewhere along the line, IT happened. Some people call it growing up, some people call it adulthood, and some people even call it gaining wisdom and insight into the way the world really works.

Whatever IT was, when IT happened, the things that once occupied hours, days, and even years of our lives faded into the abyss of adulthood, and the magic that once circled our imagination dissipated into the obscurity of reason.

Then there was Jesus. From the very beginning, Jesus defied conventional wisdom—the King of kings born in a feeding trough in a barn, certainly the last place anyone expected to find the Messiah.

Drew Dyson

Jesus' teaching did the same thing. Throughout his ministry, Jesus took the wisdom of the world he lived in and turned it on its head. The parables he told threw conventional wisdom out the window and invited his listeners to imagine a different reality.

What he said was, "The kingdom of God is like ...." What he meant was, "Imagine a world where ...."

Imagine a world where ...

- a rich man wants to throw a party and invites the poor off the streets.
- a Samaritan goes out of his way to help a Jew.
- a son, who walks away from his family and curses his father's name, is welcomed back with open arms.

Jesus' life invited the same imagination. Imagine a world where ...

- the blind receive sight and the lame are cured.
- sinners were welcomed into the presence of God's own Son.

The ultimate act of folly was the Crucifixion. The world was looking for a messiah, and the child of promise, for whom they were still holding out hope, hung nailed to a cross. And in his ultimate absurd act, Jesus laid down his life so that you and I would have eternal life.

Because Jesus so defied people's expectations of a Messiah, Paul says that the cross is a stumbling block for Jews and foolishness to the Gentiles. *No one* can believe that in this act of weakness, hopelessness, and even foolishness was the salvation of the world.

It is no wonder why Jesus said that we ought to become like little children. Only a child (or a fool) could believe that salvation would lie in the Messiah's brutal, humiliating death.

As Christians and ministers with youth, we are called to lay aside our own wisdom and dare to believe in the foolishness of God.

Thoughts for Prayer:

- Are you foolish enough to believe that God can heal the broken places of your life?
- Are you foolish enough to believe that God can heal the broken places of this world?
- Are you foolish enough to believe that Jesus Christ can take that kid who is so obviously going in the wrong direction and turn his or her life around?

50 Living the Dance: Divine Hospitality

The LORD appeared to Abraham by the oaks of Mamre, as he sat at the entrance of his tent in the heat of the day. He looked up and saw three men standing near him. When he saw them, he ran from the tent entrance to meet them, and bowed down to the ground. He said, "My lord, if I find favor with you, do not pass by your servant. Let a little water be brought, and was your feet, and rest yourselves under the tree. Let me bring a little bread, that you may refresh yourselves, and after than you may pass on —since you have come to you servant." So they said, "Do as you have said." And Abraham hastened into the tent to Sarah, and said, "Make ready quickly three measures of choice flour, knead it, and make cakes." Abraham ran to the herd, and took a calf, tender and good, and gave it to the servant, who hastened to prepare it. Then he took curds and milk and the calf that he had prepared and set it before them; and he stood by them under the tree while they ate.

They said to him, "Where is your wife Sarah?" And he said, "There, in the tent." Then one said, "I will surely return to you in due season, and your wife Sarah shall have a son." And Sarah was listening at the tent entrance behind him. Now Abraham and Sarah were old, advanced in age; it had ceased to be with Sarah after the manner of women. So Sarah laughed to herself, saying, "After I have grown old, and my husband is old, shall I have pleasure?" The LORD said to Abraham, "Why did Sarah laugh, and say, 'Shall I indeed bear a child, now that I am old?' Is anything too wonderful for the LORD? At the set time I will return to you, in due season, and Sarah shall have a son." But Sarah denied, saying, "I did not laugh"; for she was afraid. He said, "Oh yes, you did laugh."

—Genesis 18:1-15

Heather's dad had just announced to the family that he was divorcing her mother and moving to southern California with his longtime secretary. Brian was caught earlier in the week with a small amount of marijuana in his locker. Becca was in a fight with her best friend, and they hadn't been talking for several weeks. Chad was failing algebra and afraid of the repercussions that he was facing from his parents.

The question was simple enough, I thought, but the responses were far from simple. "So, how was your week?" That question opened a floodgate of emotional responses as we all sat around the chancel area talking, listening, and

Drew Dyson

praying. I was initially concerned for the new youth who had just moved into the area and was visiting the youth group for the first time. But within the first fifteen minutes, she felt comfortable talking about her fears of being in a new place and her longing to return to Pennsylvania.

It was one of those "God moments" when the unexpected happens and the sacred appears in the mundane. Years later, the students who were at youth group that night continue to talk about it as one of their favorite meetings. Discussing that one simple question was a sacred moment of divine hospitality where the sanctuary of our church was truly transformed into a sanctuary from the crushing pressures of the world.

Those opportunities for safe discussions in a safe space continue to provide a centering point for our youth ministry. In a world where teenagers face the steady drumbeat of family pressures, school struggles, and relational crises, the music of divine hospitality provides a "soul-full" interlude.

Henri Nouwen, in his book, *Reaching Out: The Three Movements of the Spiritual Life* (Image, 1986), says, "We cannot change the world by a new plan, project or idea. We cannot even change other people by our convictions, stories, advice, and proposals, but we can offer a space where people are encouraged to disarm themselves, to lay aside their occupations and preoccupations and to listen with attention and care to the voices speaking in their own center."

Teenagers live in a world where they are constantly occupied and preoccupied. Their time is occupied by sports, music lessons, school, youth group, yearbook, and family time. Their minds and hearts are preoccupied with the constant pressures and consistent struggles common to adolescence.

In my early years in youth ministry I spent a lot of time creating outrageous events that would attract young people to the church and honing talks that I would give to convince youth to commit their lives to following Christ. My intentions were rock solid, and I continue to be a strong advocate for creativity and programming in youth ministry, but the balance was off.

I realized that I was being called to live out the Christian practice of divine hospitality in youth ministry. I was being led to create a place of emptiness or nothingness in which it would be OK for young people to come and be themselves, to voice their joys and their sadness, and to set aside the pressures of the day in order to encounter the Holy One. One of my primary roles was to carve out time from the schedule and give permission for emptiness so that the divine encounter could occur, both for the youth and for myself.

Challenge: Find a creative way to carve out a space of "emptiness" in your youth ministry and practice the art of divine hospitality.

51 Prayers From the Heart

I thank my God every time I remember you,
constantly praying with joy in every one of my
prayers for all of you, because of your sharing in
the gospel from the first day until now. I am confident
of this, that the one who began a good work among you will
bring it to me to think this way about all of you, because you
hold me in your heart, for all of you share in God's grace
with me, both in my imprisonment and in the defense and
confirmation of the gospel. For God is my witness, how I long
for all of you with the compassion of Christ Jesus. And this is
my prayer, that your love may overflow more and more with
knowledge and full insight to help you to determine what is
best, so that in the day of Christ you may be pure and
blameless, having produced the harvest of righteousness that
comes through Jesus Christ for the glory and praise of God.

—Philippians 1:3-11

One of my mentors, a longtime pastor in several churches, gave me a gift on the occasion of his retirement. It was his official "ministerial record" from the course of his over forty years serving in local churches throughout our state. The record included the usual: baptisms, weddings, funerals, and appointments. But it also included a very detailed section of prayer concerns from each congregation that he served. And you could always tell when his ministry at one congregation came to a close.

The last entry from his time at each charge was a prayer written specifically for that congregation. In some places he prayed for a warm and welcoming spirit for the new pastoral family. In others he prayed for the cessation of turmoil surrounding a particular decision that had been made years earlier. In another he prayed for increased attention to the Christian education of children and youth. In all places he prayed that hearts would continue to be open to the leading of the Holy Spirit and that the parishioners would grow in their knowledge and love of God.

Throughout his letters to various churches, the Apostle Paul prays for the people in his charge. For the people of Corinth he prays for the strength and courage they need to stand blameless in God's sight. For the people of Ephesus he prays for wisdom and divine revelation so that the Ephesians might come to know the hope and riches that come through Christ Jesus. For the people of Philippi he prays that God would continue to work in their lives and that they would overflow with knowledge and love for God.

Drew Dyson

This summer, as I was reading the letters of Paul and thinking about the youth of my congregation, I gained a greater appreciation for the depth of Paul's prayers. Paul's prayers were specific to each congregation and its needs. They were prayed from the heart of a pastor who longed for his congregations to receive and understand the grace of God at work in their lives.

Any youth ministry must be built on the bedrock of prayer; and those prayers must flow from the needs of the youth and families involved. Challenge yourself to read all of Paul's prayers throughout his epistles. Note his longings, his warnings, and his encouragement. Pay attention to the depth of his concern and the passion behind his instructions.

Challenge: Think about the youth in your ministry. What would John need to help him overcome the obstacles that are keeping him from a relationship with Christ? What would Mary need in order to see God's plan for her life? What would Helen need to surmount the web of guilt over past mistakes that have ensnared her? Let your prayers for the youth in your congregation flow from your heart. Write down your prayers. Send them to youth as an offering of encouragement, a word of warning, or a prayer of thanksgiving.

52 Don't Let It Pass You By

Then Jesus said to the disciples, "There was a rich man who had a manager, and charges were brought to him that this man was squandering his property. So he summoned him and said to him, 'What is this that I hear about you? Give me an accounting of your management, because you cannot be my manager any longer.' Then the manager said to himself, 'What will I do, now that my master is taking the position away from me? I am not strong enough to dig, and I am ashamed to beg. I have decided what to do so that, when I am dismissed as manager, people may welcome me into their homes.' So, summoning his master's debtors one by one, he asked the first, 'How much do you owe my master?' He answered, 'A hundred jugs of olive oil.' He said to him, 'Take your bill, sit down quickly, and make it fifty.' Then he asked another, 'And how much do you owe?' He replied, 'A hundred containers of wheat.' He said to him, 'Take your bill and make it eighty.' And his master commended the dishonest manager because he had acted shrewdly; for the children of this age are more shrewd in dealing with their own generation than are the children of light. And I tell you, make friends for yourselves by means of dishonest wealth so that when it is gone, they may welcome you into the eternal homes.

"Whoever is faithful in a very little is faithful also in much; and whoever is dishonest in a very little is dishonest also in much."

—Luke 16:1-10 (my emphasis)

If the day could have gone by any slower it would have been yesterday. It was a late Tuesday afternoon in the middle of winter, and my phone had been ringing off the hook. One parent was upset by one of the games we had played at the retreat the weekend before. Another called to question my choice of movies for the junior high lock-in. Another well-meaning member stopped by to tell me about the mess that the youth had left in the kitchen. In addition to all of that, the bulletin material was due for Ash Wednesday, the dry cleaning had to be picked up, and I was the storyteller for my son's kindergarten class the next day and had to prepare.

The pity party began. Is this really what I went to seminary and college for? Is this what I have been praying for? Is this really ministry? I was about to pass out party favors to myself and put on the party music when the business administrator stopped in with a cup of coffee. "Perfect," I thought to myself, "nothing like company for a pity party!" She was holding a book that she had

Drew Dyson

been reading, and she had something she wanted to tell me. "I've been preparing for my Lenten Bible study and one of the parables we are talking about is the crooked manager," she said. "I came across this passage and thought it was so great that I wanted to share it with you."

Fred Craddock, in his commentary on this parable, said:

> The life of a disciple is one of faithful attention to the frequent and familiar tasks of each day, however small and insignificant they may seem. Most of us will not this week christen a ship, write a book, end a war, appoint a cabinet, dine with the queen, convert a nation, or be burned at the stake. More likely the week will present no more than a chance to give a cup of water, write a note, visit a nursing home, vote for a county commissioner, teach a Sunday school class, give our tithe, share a meal, tell a child a story, go to choir practice, and feed the neighbor's cat.[*]

"Whoever is faithful in a very little is faithful also in much; and whoever is dishonest in a very little is dishonest also in much" (verse 10).

As the business administrator walked out with coffee in hand, I began to review the events of the day. I couldn't believe all of the opportunities for ministry that had been before me that day—and all of them that I had missed. I had treated conversations with parents as annoyances and interruptions rather than as ministry opportunities. I didn't give my full attention to interactions with other staff members. I passed by children in the nursery school on my way in and kids waiting for the high school bus that I drive by every morning.

But tomorrow is another day. And with this simple reminder of the importance of faithfulness in every situation—regardless of how big or small—I will be prepared for action. Amid the busy-ness of ministry, let's not forget that each moment is an opportunity for ministry. Our faithfulness in treating each moment with care can make a significant difference in the lives of church secretaries, dry cleaners, and kindergarten students.

Challenge: Look for ways throughout this day to be a blessing to people in your path.

[*] From *Luke,* Interpretation (Louisville: Westminster/John Knox, 1990), page 192.

Contributors

<u>Drew Dyson</u> (editor and devotions 43—52) and his wife, Diane, are the adoring parents of Jeremy Stephen and Allison Taylor. His primary responsibilities include playing dinosaurs and dress-up, applying bandages to boo-boos, and long-distance driving in adverse conditions. Drew is Associate Pastor for Youth at a United Methodist church in New Jersey, and he authored *Faith-Forming Junior High Ministry* and contributed to *Soul Tending: Life-forming Practices for Older Youth and Young Adults.*

<u>Mark DeVries</u> (devotions 1—5) is associate pastor for youth and their families at First Presbyterian Church in Nashville, Tennessee, and has also led Young Life clubs. As the founder of Family Based Youth Ministry, Mark is a sought-after consultant and speaker for youth and family ministries. He lives with his wife and their three children in Nashville.

<u>Mark Schultz</u> (devotions 1—5) is an award-winning contemorary Christian recording artist. When he is home in Nashville, Tennessee, he volunteers with the youth group at First Presbyterian Church. Mark's current CD, *Stories and Songs* is in stores now.

<u>Duffy Robbins</u> (devotions 6—11) chairs the youth ministry department at Eastern College and is a member of the speaking team for Youth Specialties' National Resource Seminars. He speaks around the country at camps and conferences to both teenagers and youth workers. He's authored and co-authored numerous books, including *Memory Makers* and *Spontaneous Melodramas.*

Steve Case (devotions 12–14) has been in youth ministry for more than a dozen years. He has worked for congregations of various denominations and currently serves as youth minister at Windermere Union United Church of Christ in Florida. Steve has published several articles on creative worship ideas for teens, has taught workshops at national ministry conventions, and is the author of *The Book of Uncommon Prayer* and *Road Rules*. He lives in central Florida with his wife and two children.

Tony Jones (devotions 15–16) is presently working on his Ph.D. in Practical Theology at Princeton Theological Seminary. Previously he was the minister to youth and young adults at the Colonial Church of Edina in Minnesota for seven years. He has authored four books: *Postmodern Youth Ministry*, *Soul Shaper*, *Read.Think.Pray.Live.*, and *Pray*. Tony lives in New Jersey with his wife, Julie, and their two children, Tanner and Lily.

Kara Lassen Oliver (devotions 17–21) has been in ministry with youth for the last ten years. She has served as the program director for the former United Methodist Youth Organization and now serves as the youth pastor at Belmont United Methodist Church in Nashville, Tennessee. She lives in Nashville with her husband and daughter.

Jay Williams, (devotions 22–24) a recent graduate of Harvard University, is a strategy analyst at a Wall Street firm (go figure!). Jay is active in the ministries of The United Methodist Church, serving as a coordinator of youth and young adult ministries for his congregation in East Harlem and as director of several denominational agencies. As an activist in the modern-day abolitionist movement, Jay has twice traveled to Sudan, to help free slaves. Jay studies the "dance-fight-game" known as *capoeira*, an Afro-Brazilian martial art, and is a diehard fan of the 1980s cartoon, *Thundercats*, and MTV's *The Real World*.

Lynne Wells Graziano (devotions 25–29) resides in Roswell, Georgia, with her husband and three children. Active in youth work for ten years, she is an elder in her church, where she leads a senior high Bible study. Lynne has served as a teaching director for community Bible study, a presenter at the Youth Specialties National Youth Workers Convention, and a speaker for Cokesbury Youth Ministry Seminars. She currently freelances as a motivational speaker, retreat leader, and writer.

Will Penner (devotions 30–34) is the editor of *Youthworker Journal* and serves as the volunteer youth pastor at Westview United Methodist Church in Fairview, Tennessee. Will has taught English, creative writing, and civics in public and private high schools; he's coached debate and varsity softball; and he was even the principal of a small, Christian secondary school. Will has also served as music minister at United Methodist, Southern Baptist, and Presbyterian churches. He received his B.S.Ed. and M.S.Ed. from Baylor University, and is "all-but-dissertation" for a Ph.D. in Education and Human Development from Vanderbilt University.

Michael Hryniuk, Ph.D. (devotions 35–39), is co-director for the Youth Ministry and Spirituality Project at San Fransico Theological Seminary. He recently finished his doctoral dissertation on spiritual transformation.

Mike Baughman (devotions 40–42) is pastor for youth at a United Methodist church in New Jersey. He is passionate about helping youth discover the meaning of the sacraments and structuring the theology of youth ministry around sacraments. Mike lives with his wife in New Jersey.